For Lorraine,

May your heart be full of peace & joy this Advent season. I'm so thankful having you as my neighbor.
    Blessings,
      Lisa ♡

Awaiting HIS COMING

25 ADVENT REFLECTIONS

RHODA GRIFFIN

WESTBOW
PRESS®
A DIVISION OF THOMAS NELSON
& ZONDERVAN

Copyright © 2021 Rhoda Griffin.

All rights reserved. No part of this book may be used or reproduced by any means, graphic, electronic, or mechanical, including photocopying, recording, taping or by any information storage retrieval system without the written permission of the author except in the case of brief quotations embodied in critical articles and reviews.

WestBow Press books may be ordered through booksellers or by contacting:

WestBow Press
A Division of Thomas Nelson & Zondervan
1663 Liberty Drive
Bloomington, IN 47403
www.westbowpress.com
844-714-3454

Because of the dynamic nature of the Internet, any web addresses or links contained in this book may have changed since publication and may no longer be valid. The views expressed in this work are solely those of the author and do not necessarily reflect the views of the publisher, and the publisher hereby disclaims any responsibility for them.

Any people depicted in stock imagery provided by Getty Images are models, and such images are being used for illustrative purposes only. Certain stock imagery © Getty Images.

Scripture quotations are from the ESV® Bible (The Holy Bible, English Standard Version®), copyright © 2001 by Crossway, a publishing ministry of Good News Publishers. Used by permission. All rights reserved.

Scripture quotations marked (NLT) are taken from the Holy Bible, New Living Translation, copyright ©1996, 2004, 2015 by Tyndale House Foundation. Used by permission of Tyndale House Publishers, a Division of Tyndale House Ministries, Carol Stream, Illinois 60188. All rights reserved.

Scripture quotations taken from The Holy Bible, New International Version® NIV® Copyright © 1973 1978 1984 2011 by Biblica, Inc. TM. Used by permission. All rights reserved worldwide.

Scripture taken from the New King James Version® Copyright © 1982 by Thomas Nelson. Used by permission. All rights reserved.

Scripture taken from the King James Version of the Bible.

ISBN: 978-1-6642-5060-4 (sc)
ISBN: 978-1-6642-5062-8 (hc)
ISBN: 978-1-6642-5061-1 (e)

Library of Congress Control Number: 2021923702

Print information available on the last page.

WestBow Press rev. date: 11/24/2021

Contents

Acknowledgments ix

Preface xi
You Are Invited to Wait with Me

Day 1 1
Let Every Heart Prepare Him Room

Day 2 5
The Longing

Day 3 9
Arise! Shine! For Your Light Has Come!

Day 4 13
Emmanuel, God with Us

Day 5 17
The Place with a Past

Day 6 21
The Novel Noel

Day 7 25
The Courageous God

Day 8 31
FEAR NOT

Day 9 37
SHOW ME YOUR GLORY

Day 10 41
GOD'S INTERRUPTIONS

Day 11 45
THE GIFT-WRAPPED LAMB

Day 12 49
IN SEARCH OF THE KING

Day 13 53
THE GREATEST GIFT

Day 14 59
FALL ON YOUR KNEES

Day 15 63
GREAT EXPECTATIONS

Day 16 67
THE QUEEN AND HER KING

Day 17 73
A SON GIVEN

Day 18 79
THE ACCESSIBLE GOD

Day 19 85
THE FATHER GOD

Day 20 91
PRINCE OF PEACE

Day 21 97
THE STAR AND THE SCEPTER

Day 22 103
THE ROOT-SHOOT

Day 23 109
THE LION LAMB

Day 24 115
JOY TO THE WORLD

Day 25 121
COME AND SEE WHAT GOD HAS DONE

Notes 125

Acknowledgments

I would like to thank my husband, Lucas Griffin, who faithfully edited my reflections each night before I shared them daily and caught all those little technicalities. Also thanks to Kyle Fairfield, who was my doctrinal filter. Not sure how many times I requested a read-through at ten at night. Thanks to all my precious friends who encouraged me to step out in faith and prayed for me throughout the weeks, particularly to Sheila Hanet, Karen Voisin, and Lana Lander, as well as my sisters, Priscilla Griffin and Mareshah McCammon. Your support was so appreciated. And thanks to all of you for joining me on this venture! It is so nice to be "traveling in company." Last and certainly not least, my greatest thanks goes to the Lord for creating this vision and then unrolling it before me, one day at a time. What a blessing He has been to my soul!

Preface

You Are Invited to Wait with Me

Dear Friend,

This series of reflections was born one Advent season out of a deep longing to find some light in a dark time. The entire world had been traveling through a very trying year during 2020, and November fell heavily upon us all. My heart sighed beneath the weight, and as we approached December, I began to reach for Christ, almost in desperation, as a means to ward off the despair. The words first came as a whisper into my soul, "Awaiting His Coming." I didn't know the fullness of what they meant, other than to understand that, yes, I was indeed awaiting Him and His presence this year especially. I was waiting on Him deeply. Christmas—that time of year when the world collectively remembers His birth—was just a month away, and so these words made sense within that context. As a believer, I do not depend on just one season to inspire my celebration of Christ's birth, but I am grateful that the greater world still pauses at the memory of His first coming. So my heart was open to awaiting Him.

I decided I would lean into the waiting with all of my heart. I unplugged media, spurned my phone, opened my Bible wide, pulled out the commentaries and Bible study tools, and cranked the carols. And in my own way, I rebelled against the doom and gloom by triumphing in His light. I wept my way through December, not in sorrow, but in the overwhelming joy of Christ's first Advent and the hope of His second, which we continue to wait for and pray is not a distant event. Each day, the Scriptures breathed their life, hope, peace, joy, and love into my spirit—all the candles of Advent. The Lord struck me time and again with new visions of Himself. I was in awe and knew I was treading on holy ground. Just when I thought I had received the greatest treasure, I would open His Word the following day, only to unearth another. The thoughts just kept on coming. Each day, sometimes even into the night, He poured out His gems, Himself, to me.

Initially, I had intended to make the journey alone—to listen and journal, await and enjoy Him all to myself. But the Lord had something else in mind. He wanted me to share the wealth. And I can only describe it as a wind at my back, a gentle nudging, pushing me along, pressing me to open up the treasure box and share my discoveries with others. I am a shy writer and tend to privately share my writings. To open up and publically share this journey was going to require a huge step of faith for this timid author—not to mention the required faith to believe that the Lord would provide something for me each and every day once I made the commitment to share something daily.

I took a deep breath and sent out this invitation to family and friends via email and social media (the only activity I would have on social media all month would be to post these reflections). I posted the following invitation:

> I don't know about you, but after coming through a year like the one we have just been through, I know I could sure use some hope and light this Christmas season! Please join me December 1–25 for a daily series of Advent reflections I am calling

"Awaiting His Coming." These words have been running through my mind for weeks now, and I have felt pressed at the close of this year to live immersed in the hope and light that Jesus brings during the season named for Him, CHRISTmas.

Of course, every day of the year I look to Christ for hope and light, but this month I plan to especially surround myself with the promises of Scripture that point towards His first coming, as well as to step meaningfully into the details surrounding His birth. So for each day from December 1–25, I will share a brief reflection as we move closer to His coming, and if you are also encouraged as a result, then it will be well worth this undertaking that is encouraging me forward. You are welcome to join me as I await His coming. Would you wait with me too? No pressure at all, this is merely an invitation. I look forward to waiting with you these next few weeks …

And the invitation still holds! We still await His coming. Each and every year, we celebrate His first coming and await His return. Please join me over these next few weeks, and may you too be blessed in the waiting.

1
DAY

Let Every Heart Prepare Him Room

> She ... laid him in a manger, because there
> was no room for them in the inn.
> —Luke 2:7 (NKJV)

Even as a child, these words broke my heart. Maybe *because* I was a child, they broke my heart. I remember watching plays of the nativity throughout my childhood and always feeling a pang of shame on behalf of humankind for turning the unborn Christ away, along with His heavily pregnant mother and her most likely desperate husband. The cruel irony, that the One who always makes room for us could find no one to make room for Him, still tears at my heart. This trend would follow Him throughout His life, such that Jesus Himself said, "Foxes have dens and birds of the air have nests, but the Son of Man has no place to lay his head" (Luke 9:58 NIV). He would be, as the prophet Isaiah foretold, One who was "despised and rejected" (Isaiah 53:3 NKJV) and One who "came to His own, and His own people did not receive Him" (John 1:11 ESV). But who could have anticipated that the rejection would start so early?

Certainly, there were extenuating circumstances that created a shortage of space in Bethlehem that night. Caesar's census had required each person to return to the town of his heritage, and one can imagine that all the small towns were bursting at the seams with travelers. A nation known for its hospitality was being stretched to its capacity and pushed to the limit of its show of courtesy. Perhaps the turning away of this unborn guest was not meant out of spite but more out of inconvenience and a sense of inadequacy. Yet the foreshadowing is unmistakable. Jesus was already being pushed into the margins, into the outside place, away with the animals, where a food trough would become His bed. I could just cry. Imagine it: Jesus had not even been born yet, and He was already being turned away.

This begs the question "Do I have any room for Jesus?"

In the craziness of life, which especially seems to mount during the Christmas season, do I get so overwhelmed that I turn Christ away? Do I have any room left in my life for Jesus? Is there still a place within my heart for Him? Will I "prepare Him room" during this Christmas season? Or do I find Him to be an inconvenience? A hassle? An obligatory extra? Am I already "at capacity" with the demands, the people, and the parties? Is my "inn" already full? And if I should let Him in, would He inevitably remain in an outside place, not central to my life or this season I am in? Perhaps it is not that I wish Him ill, but I just really could not be bothered to make space for Him. He would be just one more thing in a list of too many things already.

Friend, Jesus is not a burdensome guest.

And I think we stumble on this point. In our experience, hosting means added pressure and strain. How often do we stress over the work of hosting only to lose sight of the joy a guest can bring?

Guests are work, without a doubt. It exhausts me to think of all the ways in which I prepare for a guest, beginning with a deep clean of my home from top to bottom. We're not talking a cursory whisk around the living room. We're talking a rearrange-the-furniture kind of clean. A no-one-must-know-that-we-live-here kind of clean! Junk goes in the trash, and everything in my path is destined for a purging. Nothing is sacred, my kids have learned. Remote corners are attacked with a vengeance, chairs are stacked, couches are moved, and cleaning supplies that haven't seen the light of day for months are thrown into work. Then there's the guestroom to set up, possibly resulting in a child inconveniently ousted from her room to bunk in with siblings. Sheets are washed, beds made up, and towels laid out. There're the meal planning, grocery shopping, baking, cooking—oh, I almost forgot the added expense. There goes my "new dryer" fund. Is this guest really worth it?

We need to stop. *Just. Stop.*

Jesus isn't that kind of guest. He doesn't need you or your life to be perfect in order for you to make room for Him. He isn't coming to see your couch. He's coming to see you. Your drapes neither distract Him nor impress Him. He's here to fellowship with you. You just simply need to open your door. Just reach for the handle, turn the knob, and take the step of welcoming Him in. Receive Him right where He finds you. In your mess. In the disaster. In your chaos. In the fear. In your anxiety. In the broken pieces. In your "not enoughs" and "what ifs." Let Him into whatever your life is right now. He'll do the rest. He'll be your cleanup crew. He'll rearrange the furniture. (Oh, let me tell you He will.) He'll find His way around just fine. Don't you worry about a thing. Just let Him into your home, into your heart, and into your life. Welcome Him. Make a place for Him. Sit down with Him. Enjoy Him. That's what it means to prepare Him room—to spend time with Him, rest in Him, and enjoy His company.

Jesus once had to correct Martha for her frantic take on hosting Him. While her sister, Mary, sat at Jesus's feet, drinking in His presence and leaning into His every word, Martha hustled about the house trying to perfect every detail from the décor to the meal. When she tossed up her arms in complaint, Jesus replied, "Martha, Martha … you are worried and upset about many things, but few things are needed—or indeed only one. Mary has chosen what is better, and it will not be taken away from her" (Luke 10:41–42 NIV). Maybe you and I need to replace our own name with Martha's, remember "what is better," and recall the only thing that we truly need is His presence.

So today He is standing outside your heart's door, just as He stood outside of the church at Laodicea, calling you from your lukewarm affection for Him and your casual attitude toward Him, alerting you to your great need of His transforming power, inviting you to open to Him. "Behold, I stand at the door and knock. If anyone hears My voice and opens the door, I will come in to him and dine with him, and he with Me" (Revelation 3:20 NKJV). Do you hear His knock? Do you hear His voice? He is no longer the unborn babe quietly awaiting your response. He is now the Risen Savior, your Redeemer, your Lord. He longs for fellowship with you and desires your company. And He asks that you open to Him as a guest and a friend—that you *prepare Him room*.

You'll soon discover He's no ordinary, cumbersome, passing guest. He's one who comes to dwell with you. And once you let Him in, you will never want Him to leave.

P.S. Double-check your title deed. It just might have His name on it.

> Joy to the world! The Lord is come.
> Let earth receive her King.
> Let ev'ry heart prepare Him room.

DAY 2

The Longing

> At that time there was a man in Jerusalem named Simeon. He was righteous and devout and was eagerly waiting for the Messiah to come and rescue Israel.
> —Luke 2:25 (NLT)

> She [Anna] talked about the child to everyone who had been waiting expectantly for God to rescue Jerusalem.
> —Luke 2:38 (NLT)

The anticipation of an arrival!

Whether it be that close friend coming to visit, one's precious child returning home, or a newborn gracing the family, so much *longing* is measured in a coming.

And if there were one underlying tone to what I am feeling these days, it could be summed up in this word: *longing*.

All the aching of humanity, all the sighs of a broken world, all its hurting people, and all the damage sin has done create within me so much yearning for the way it's supposed to be, craving for the day it *will* be, and, at risk of sounding cliché, desire for some peace, love, and joy for our world. Surely, I am not alone in this longing.

The story of God's ancient people, Israel, is also one of longing. They longed to see God's promises come to pass: the promise of God's salvation and a Savior; the promise of the Messiah, the Anointed One; the promise of a King, David's offspring. And they anticipated this Promised One with great expectation.

My mind travels back to those faithful men and women who awaited the coming Messiah. How many times could they be found scanning the horizon for the Chosen One?

Generations came and went, yet the writer to the Hebrews tells us, "All these people died still believing what God had promised them. They did not receive what was promised, but they saw it all from a distance and welcomed it" (Hebrews 11:13 NLT). Though Jesus Christ did not come in their time, by faith, they saw His coming and joyfully embraced it. Jesus reflected on this joy when He said, "Your father Abraham rejoiced as he looked forward to my coming. He saw it and was glad" (John 8:56 NLT). Strange how longing can be filled with so much yearning on one hand yet so much joy on the other.

In Jesus's day, there were still those longing to see God's salvation. Maybe over the drawn-out centuries leading up to Christ, many had given up the wait. Not Simeon. Not Anna. Both eagerly awaited the Messiah.

When Simeon met the eight-day-old Jesus in the temple, he praised God, saying, "Lord … my eyes have seen your salvation that you have prepared in the presence of all peoples" (Luke 2:29–31 ESV). Similarly, Zechariah praised God "because he has visited and redeemed his people. He has sent us a mighty Savior from the royal line of his servant David, just as he promised through his holy prophets long ago" (Luke 1:68–70 NLT).

How blessed are we to live at a time when the promise of the Christ has been met? Jesus Himself once said, "I tell you the truth, many prophets and righteous people longed to see what you see, but they didn't see it. And they longed to hear what you hear, but they didn't hear it" (Matthew 13:17 NLT).

So where does this leave us? Living well beyond the time of Christ, satisfied with His salvation of our souls, and yet still yearning for the full redemption of all creation? That longing remains because we are those caught in the dash between His first and second coming. By faith, we have received many of the promises found in Him, and yet even we await still more promises to come in a future time when He will reign eternally as King. He won't be what He is now—the rejected Messiah, received only by a few believing hearts. He will be the reigning Messiah—recognized for the Sovereign King that He is, ruling in righteousness and at last bringing to our poor, broken world, all the peace, love, and joy it longs for. That, my friend, is the longing you and I feel.

This is why we await His coming. His first coming holds us in awe of a God who would willingly step from the perfections of heaven into the squalor of a barn (a vague reflection of the greater world beyond) to fulfill His long-ago promises to His people. And His coming again calls to our hearts with hope for the promises He has yet to fulfill.

So, in the madness of the world in which we live, the haste and pace of the eleven months that are behind us, at last we move into a month at the close of the year, and just for a season, we collectively pour out all our longing and await His coming. We mark a pause in our lives to stop and reflect upon the arrival of the Savior of the world and imagine our future with our coming King!

> O Come, O Come, Emmanuel
> And ransom captive Israel
> That mourns in lowly exile here
> Until the Son of God appear.
> Rejoice! Rejoice! Emmanuel
> Shall come to thee, O Israel

DAY 3

Arise! Shine! For Your Light Has Come!

Arise, shine; for your light has come! And the glory of the Lord is risen upon you. For behold, the darkness shall cover the earth, and deep darkness the people; but the Lord will arise over you, and His glory will be seen upon you.
—Isaiah 60:1–2 (NKJV)

The people who walked in darkness have seen a great light; those who dwelt in a land of deep darkness, on them has light shone.
—Isaiah 9:2 (ESV)

The people dwelling in darkness have seen a great light, and for those dwelling in the region and shadow of death, on them a light has dawned.
—Matthew 4:16 (ESV)

> Because of the tender mercy of our God, whereby sunrise shall visit us from on high to give light to those who sit in darkness and in the shadow of death, to guide our feet into the way of peace.
> —Luke 1:78–79 (ESV)

I dread the plunging darkness as we move into winter, the long nights and short days with the sun slipping away far too soon—liquid gold sliding through our fingers and shadows closing the day as soon as it has passed its zenith. Long, cold, bitter months of winter stretched out before us. That time of year when night rules the land.

Shiver.

Night also ruled the land of Israel into which Jesus was born. Merciless, chronic, deep darkness spread like a plague, and no one escaped its effect.

Not the kind of night in which there is an absence of the sun.

The kind of night in which there is an absence of the Son.

The sort of night that comes from "trouble and anguish and dark despair" (Isaiah 8:22 NLT).

The world Jesus entered was not a far cry from the shadow of death. Listen to the language of their circumstances—they "dwelled in a land of deep darkness" (Isaiah 9:2 ESV) in "the region where death casts its shadow" (Matthew 4:16 NLT). Oppressed by Roman masters, overwhelmed by man-made religious laws, and blinded by sin and suffering, these people suffocated beneath the heaviness of it all.

I don't know what your situation is today. I don't know the night you're living or what darkness has fallen over your life or which shadows have cast their despair across your path. I don't know the state of your health, your wealth, your family relationships, or what else threatens to stifle you. I don't know what's breaking your heart or crushing your spirit.

Deeper still, I don't know the state of your soul—the unconfessed wrongs, the choking bitterness, the faithless fretting, the cherished sins. I don't know your soul … but I do know mine. And I know that the night within can be darker than the night without—more in need of the light of Christ than the light of day, requiring His brightness more than the circumstances in which we are found. And it is for this reason that we desperately depend upon the Sonrise of the Savior and the birth of Christ within our hearts.

The night in which these people lived was spiritual night—piercing, perpetual, pervading darkness. They stumbled through their lives, as we do ours, under the pressure of it, maybe completely unaware that this is not the way things are supposed to be. But then again, maybe they were waking up from that sleep to the dawning that there must be more to life than this death they were living.

To these weary ones, the startling message of hope came: "Arise, shine; for your light has come!" (Isaiah 60:1 NKJV).

Everything was about to change! Just when they thought there was no way out. Just when all hope for the morning was lost. Just when despair threatened to take hold and they couldn't live this way a moment longer …

A great light appeared! The light dawned on their darkness with the birth of Jesus Christ and shone into its furthest corners. And the darkness didn't stand a chance.

The darkness never stands a chance when met with light. Light, by its very nature, conquers whatever darkness it meets and always dispels the gloom. As Andrew Peterson says in his song, "Is He Worthy?": "All the dark won't stop the light from getting through."[1]

In his gospel, John tells us, "The light shines in the darkness, and the darkness has not overcome it … The true light, which gives light to everyone, was coming into the world" (John 1:5, 9 ESV). And it is Jesus Christ who clarifies that He is "the light of the world" (John 9:5 ESV).

He came. He shone. He conquered!

Christ shines into your darkness too. All of it. Every degree, every layer, every shade of night. Every corner of your heart and life, He shines! And like a beacon of hope, He proclaims, "I am the light of the world. Whoever follows me will not walk in darkness, but will have the light of life" (John 8:12 ESV).

The light is calling, my friend, awakening us with its indomitable command: "Arise, shine; for your light has come! And the glory of the Lord is risen upon you" (Isaiah 60:1 NKJV). It's time to step from darkness into light. It's time to embrace His light and discover that "Christ will shine on you" (Ephesians 5:14 ESV) to the dawning of a new day.

> O come, Thou Day-Spring, come and cheer
> Our spirits by Thine advent here
> Disperse the gloomy clouds of night
> And death's dark shadows put to flight
> Rejoice! Rejoice, Emmanuel
> Shall come to thee, O Israel
>
> Long lay the world in sin and error pining
> Till He appeared and the soul felt its worth
> A thrill of hope, the weary world rejoices
> For yonder breaks, a new and glorious morn

DAY

Emmanuel, God with Us

All this took place to fulfill what the Lord had spoken by the prophet: "Behold, the virgin shall conceive and bear a son, and they shall call his name Immanuel" (which means, God with us).
—Matthew 1:22–23 (ESV)

Therefore the Lord himself will give you a sign. Behold, the virgin shall conceive and bear a son, and shall call his name Immanuel.
—Isaiah 7:14 (ESV)

One of the saddest misconceptions about God is to think that He is *not* with us, that He is distant from us, He is against us, and He doesn't care about us.

Someone looks at the turmoil in our world and declares, "God is not with us." Another stands in a death camp and mourns, "God is not with us." Someone's addicted child roams the streets at night—"God is not with us." Another's spouse walks out after thirty years, and she weeps, "God is not with us." A nation's God is silent for four hundred years, and they groan, "God is not with us." From the ruin, from the rubble, from the wreckage, the cry of humanity resounds to the sky and pounds on heaven's door: "God—is—not—with—us!"

"Are you there, God? Where are you? I can't see you! Do you see me?"

This angst does not question if God exists; it wonders if God even cares. It doesn't inquire whether God *is*; it doubts whether God is present. Is He with us? Because if He were, then why wouldn't He do something about all the brokenness? Why does He not fix things? Based only on the mess I see within and without, I have nothing left except to assume that God is not with us.

Nothing dispels this despairing lie like the incarnation of Emmanuel, God with Us.

Yes, the God "who is high and lifted up, who inhabits eternity, whose name is Holy" (Isaiah 57:15 ESV) *is with us*! This same One, who lives in perfect light and dwells in a place untouched by the ravages of sin, is with us. This One, who we presume wants nothing to do with us, is Emmanuel, the God who came to us as Jesus Christ. Listen further to God's desire for us: "I live in the high and holy place *with those* whose spirits are contrite and humble. I restore the crushed spirit of the humble and revive the courage of those with repentant hearts" (Isaiah 57:15 NLT, my emphasis added). This great and awesome God *does* see our anguished spirits. He *does* live within repentant hearts. He *does* restore what is crushed by sin. He *does* care about our failing courage. He *is* with us! Not absent from us. Not distant but near. Not against us but for us.

God has forever longed to be with us. His position in highest heaven has never deterred this desire, nor has it kept Him from coming to us right where we were as humankind. King David wondered at this longing of God's when he wrote Psalm 8: "O Lord, our Lord, your majestic name fills the earth! Your glory is higher than the heavens ... What are mere mortals that you should think about them, human beings that you should care for them?" (Psalm 8:1, 4 NLT).

God cares so deeply, in fact, that He bridged the divide and closed the gap between us in the sending of His Son. Nothing could speak louder for God's desire to be with us than the gift of Emmanuel, *God with us*. He intentionally took on human form in order that He might "understand our weaknesses" and "faced all the same testings we do, yet he did not sin" (Hebrews 4:15 NLT). As a human, He understands all we endure and every hardship of our experience. "He was … a man of suffering, and familiar with pain" (Isaiah 53:3 NIV). And like the words of "O Holy Night": "He knows our need, to our weakness no stranger."

> He is *God with us* in the fatigue and exhaustion of our long days.
> *God with us* at the sick beds and gravesides of our loved ones.
> *God with us* in the hectic pace of daily life.
> *God with us* in the schoolroom or at the office.
> *God with us* in our physical agony.
> *God with us* in the emotional hurt.
> *God with us* in rejection and humiliation.
> *God with us* in our abandonment and betrayal.
> *God with us* in the hard conversations.
> *God with us* when we're misunderstood and misjudged.
> *God with us* when they insult us and treat us badly.
> *God with us* in our poverty.
> *God with us* when we wipe away the tears.
> *God with us* when we are underappreciated.
> *God with us* in the sorrow of deep loss.
> *God with us* when we're hated and threatened.
> *God with us* when we are abused.
> *God with us* in the aching loneliness.

On every human level, Emmanuel was *God with us*, and "It was necessary for him to be made in every respect like us, his brothers and sisters, so that he could be our merciful and faithful high priest before God" (Hebrews 2:17 NLT). You only truly identify with someone once you've walked a mile in his or her shoes. Jesus walked a lifetime in ours. And He still is God with us even today. Not just able to understand us, but also the only One to show up when no one else will or can, the only One to walk with us down certain roads we would otherwise travel alone, the only One to turn to when no one else can provide comfort.

But there is a deeper sense in which God is with us. He went further than just human sympathy to secure His place with us forever. *God with us* is not just a matter of *Him* being with *us*. It also involves *us* being with *Him*. He had to remove the barrier of our sin preventing *us* from being with *Him*. He could have done all that He did in becoming God with us in human form, but if He hadn't taken that vital step of accomplishing our salvation, there is no way we could be with Him. So, "Christ also suffered once for our sins ... that he might bring us to God" (1 Peter 3:18 ESV). And now God is able to make His home with us (John 14:23) and live within us forever (John 14:16). Soon we will go to be with Him where He is, according to His own desire (John 17:24), to an eternal home where "God's home is now among his people! He will live with them, and they will be his people. God himself will be with them. He will wipe every tear from their eyes, and there will be no more death or sorrow or crying or pain. All these things are gone forever" (Revelation 21:3–4 NLT). God with us. Us with God.

And so Matthew beautifully bookends his gospel with Emmanuel, in His birth at the beginning, and in His promise at the close: "And be sure of this: *I am with you* always, even to the end of the age" (Matthew 28:20 NLT, my emphasis added).

> O holy child of Bethlehem
> Descend to us we pray
> Cast out our sin and enter in
> Be born in us today ...
> Oh come to us, abide with us
> Our Lord, Emmanuel

DAY 5

The Place with a Past

> But you, O Bethlehem Ephrathah, who are too little
> to be among the clans of Judah, from you shall come
> forth for me one who is to be ruler in Israel, whose
> coming forth is from old, from ancient days.
> —Micah 5:2 (ESV)

For a town that is "too little," Bethlehem sure has a *big* history.

Its background comes rich with drama, ranging from the elation of a king's coronation to the devastating slaughter of innocent babes. Its past lays torn between great joy and gripping sorrow.

So why Bethlehem? What's the story here?

On one hand, Bethlehem tells a sorrowful tale. The first time we enter Bethlehem on the pages of Scripture in Genesis 35 is to bury Rachel, who had died between Ramah and Bethlehem while giving birth to Benoni, which means "son of my sorrow." Benoni is soon renamed Benjamin, which means "son of my right hand," but Rachel's first naming casts a dark shadow over Bethlehem. This sorrow is drawn upon in Jeremiah's prophecy: "This is what the Lord says: 'A cry is heard in Ramah—deep anguish and bitter weeping. Rachel weeps for her children, refusing to be comforted—for her children are gone'" (Jeremiah 31:15 NLT).

Jeremiah's prophecy plays out in the terrifying events that follow Jesus's birth and flight from Herod the Great, who sought to kill the newborn King:

> Then Herod, when he saw that he had been tricked by the wise men, became furious, and he sent and killed all the male children in Bethlehem and in all that region who were two years old or under, according to the time that he had ascertained from the wise men. Then was fulfilled what was spoken by the prophet Jeremiah. (Matthew 2:16–17 ESV)

O, the anguish! The horror that Bethlehem and Ramah endured! Their pain—too much to bear. Mothers weeping bitterly, refusing to be comforted. Imagine the heart-rending trauma and loss. It's unfathomable! What agony the ruthless jealousy of a wicked king brought to pass. I can hardly move past this …

But we need the complete history to make sense of the pain. So, after Rachel's death, the next time we arrive at Bethlehem in our Bibles, there is a famine in the land. Ironically, *Bethlehem* means "house of bread," and yet it is devoid of bread. So, a family of four from Bethlehem leaves the "house of bread" in search of sustenance elsewhere and settles in Moab. Tragically, the wife, Naomi, loses her husband and two sons to death. Her departure from Bethlehem has resulted in bitter disappointment.

She returns empty-handed to Bethlehem at the news that God has visited His people with bread, meaning the famine is now over. Her beloved daughter-in-law, Ruth, accompanies her, having embraced Naomi's God and people, and through a series of events, she marries the wealthy Bethlehemite Boaz. Their great-grandson would become King David. Undeserving as Naomi was, God redeemed what was lost with the birth of Ruth and Boaz's son and turned Naomi's bitterness to great joy.

This brings us to Bethlehem's royal past. In spite of the tragic history surrounding Bethlehem, it is also a place that brings much joy. As the birthplace of the great King David, it was here David tended his father's sheep until he was subsequently anointed king of Israel. So, it is no surprise to us then that our final stop in Bethlehem should bring us to the birth of a greater King, "Jesus Christ, the son of David" (Matthew 1:1 ESV).

Joseph and Mary returned "to Judea, to the city of David, which is called Bethlehem" (Luke 2:4 ESV), and "Jesus was born in Bethlehem of Judea ... for so it was written by the prophet: 'And you, O Bethlehem, in the land of Judah, are by no means least among the rulers of Judah; for from you shall come a ruler who will shepherd my people Israel'" (Matthew 2:1, 5–6 ESV).

Later in His lifetime, Jesus asked, "Has not the Scripture said that Christ comes from the offspring of David, and comes from Bethlehem, the village where David was?" (John 7:42 ESV). O little town of Bethlehem, what hope has risen from your ashes! To witness the birth of the King of kings, whose coming forth is more ancient than you!

I must say, at first when I began to sift through the history of Bethlehem, my heart was broken to reimagine the sorrow experienced within its streets—the death, starvation, and agonizing devastation. I wasn't sure how God could redeem such a past. I really had my doubts. But then as I followed the history of Christ's ancestral hometown and David's lineage leading to the birth of the great King of kings, Jesus Christ, I saw God's redemptive plan begin to take shape. And I learned some truths that turn everything on end.

In the places where our greatest night prevails, God shines His greater light, Jesus Christ.

In the places where our deepest sorrow—our Benoni—kills us,

God resurrects hope through the "Son of His right hand," Jesus Christ.

In the places of enormous loss, God restores infinite riches in Jesus Christ.

In the places where we long for a redo, God brings forth a Redeemer, Jesus Christ.

In the places where we fall short with lack, God gifts us all we need with His "living bread" (John 6:51 ESV), Jesus Christ.

In the places of our bitterest disappointments, God creates a brighter future in Jesus Christ.

My friend, God always births greatest life in the places of greatest death.

It's as Lauren Daigle's song, "How Can It Be," goes:

> Though I fall, You can make me new
> From this death I will rise with You
> Oh, the grace reaching out for me
> How can it be?[2]

History is never tidy and straightforward. In fact, it is often messy and ugly. But our past, with all its pain and drama, can be redeemed by God. And therein lies our hope—the hope of Jesus Christ, the great Redeemer of Bethlehem.

> Oh little town of Bethlehem, how still we see thee lie
> Above thy deep and dreamless sleep the silent stars go by
> Yet in thy dark streets shineth, the everlasting light
> The hopes and fears of all the years are met in thee tonight.

DAY

The Novel Noel

> But when the fullness of time had come, God sent forth His Son, born of woman, under the law, to redeem those who were under the law, so that we might receive adoption as sons.
> —Galatians 4:4–5 (ESV)

Timing is everything. It's a universal truth, especially laid bare in the telling of a joke. I don't even bother telling jokes anymore, I'm so terrible at it. It's one of those inherent skills—you either got it, or you don't. And I don't. My timing is horribly off. I can't build a thing toward a punch line. Sometimes I have to repeat or explain the punch line. Oh groan. Forget it! It's best to recognize one's deficiencies and just move on.

But what I'm talking about today is no joke.

I'm going to go with … epic novel.

And the ability to create, write, and tell an epic story is also inherent. You either got it, or you don't. And God has got it. Nailed.

You know, there's patience to be had in the planning of an epic story. There's plot structure mapped to the minutest detail, the clever dovetailing of key events, and the expert layering of significant themes.

There's characterization and development, because we all know, people make the story. There are motifs and tone and mood to consider, which amplify meaning and extend the story beyond itself—a rich blend of all the essential literary elements you thought you left behind in high school English class.

Some of us only have it in us to read, hmmm, maybe a brief poem? Ten lines max. Okay, a haiku, and we're out. Some go for the short story. Forget poetry, give 'em prose, but make it quick, or they're gone. Most go straight to the movie version. Anybody?

Not God though. Nope. Oh, He'll write poetry, to be sure. He has a few book lengths of those. And He's brilliant at the short story—impactful, eventful, concise. But what's His real specialty? What does He especially gun for? What keeps Him from settling with short, sweet, and to the point?

The epic story.

Bigger than time! Filling eternity! Oh yes, God's in it for the long haul. He is the great Novelist of time and eternity, Master of literature, Architect of the epic tale.

In fact, such is His genius, that all other heroic classics are modeled after His. For sure, it's all there. He sets the scene at creation. The inciting moment—sin enters the world through the deceit of the antagonist. The rising action climbs over centuries of promises and covenants made and covers the forging of a nation through whom all the world would be blessed. Then it moves toward the climax of the Messiah's coming—launching our hero on the journey involving His birth, life, death, resurrection, and ascension and the recreation of an apocalyptic world. And now for the denouement, the resolution, when at last we arrive at the grand conclusion, which *begins* His eternal reign.

Yes, God plays the long game. He takes pleasure in the slow telling of His tale. One must find a comfortable place to settle in for the listening. One can almost sense God lean in with the enthrallment of it all as He arrives at the climax of His story, at just the precise moment when the exact time has come for the Messiah to appear: "When the right time came, God sent his Son, born of a woman, subject to the law. God sent him to buy freedom for us who were slaves" (Galatians 4:4–5 NLT).

Why was this the right moment? What determined this to be "the right time" (Galatians 4:4 NLT)? How was this point in history the one to make the cut?

In truth, the answers are beyond our knowing as to why God determined *this* to be the time to send His Son, but there are a few clues given to us in Scripture to help us make sense of God's timing.

Adam—Luke's gospel traces Jesus's genealogy all the way back to Adam, reminding us that this moment had been building since the very beginning, indeed, even since *before* the beginning, because Luke actually takes us all the way back to "Adam, the son of God" (Luke 3:38 ESV). For centuries, God had been shaping world history through the rise and fall of its kingdoms and nations—including the dominating Roman Empire of Jesus's day—in preparation for the coming of His Son to restore what Adam had lost by sin. God prepared this time as perfect for the birth of Jesus Christ, His eventual death by Roman crucifixion, the formation of His church, and the spread of the gospel through an established world empire. In so many ways, the world was just sitting ripe for the Savior.

Abraham—Reaching back to God's covenant with Abraham, the time had come to honor it and bless all the world through Abraham's offspring, Jesus Christ.

Moses—In the verses preceding today's text, Paul compares the Jewish nation to children under the guard of Moses's law "until the date set by his father" when they would mature in Christ as fully grown sons and heirs (Galatians 4:2 NLT). Christ came as the One who would fulfill all the requirements of the law and then bear away its death penalty by His own death on the cross, allowing them to become God's sons. God's perfect timing turned them, and us, from slaves of the law to sons in Christ.

David—God was finally ready to introduce the Person who would fulfill His promise to David that one of his descendants would sit upon his throne forever. In Matthew's "genealogy of Jesus Christ, the son of David" (Matthew 1:1 ESV), he lists fourteen generations, which covers God's covenant with Abraham, the law given by Moses, and the inception of David's kingdom.

Matthew then lists another fourteen generations from David to Josiah, which takes Israel from the godly reign of King David through the glorious reign of King Solomon and then follows the nation's sad decline and departure from God in the subsequent reigns of the kings until at last God sends the nation into exile.

Matthew completes his final list of fourteen generations, which records the last sitting king when the kingdom is lost and then makes its way down a lineup of would-be kings to precisely the fourteenth generation with the birth of Jesus Christ. It's as though God was unwilling to let even one more generation pass without fulfilling His promise of a King who would sit on David's throne forever. God's impeccable timing.

So, the fullness of time had come for both God and humanity in the birth of Jesus Christ, who is the climax of history, who fulfilled all the promises and covenants God had made, and who established God's everlasting kingdom.

Timing is everything. It's a universal truth, especially laid bare in the telling of His story ...

> Late in time behold Him come
> Offspring of a Virgin's womb ...
> Glory to the newborn King!

DAY 7

The Courageous God

> Christ Jesus ... though he was God, he did not think of equality with God as something to cling to. Instead, he gave up his divine privileges; he took the humble position of a slave and was born as a human being. When he appeared in human form, he humbled himself by becoming obedient to the point of death, even death on a cross.
> —Philippians 2:5–8 (NLT)

Jesus didn't have to come.

I know, I know, the Father sent the Son. But the Father and the Son were one on this, united in purpose, perfectly blended in will. Jesus Christ knowingly, willingly, and unhesitatingly *chose* to come. His arrival was very much on purpose. He intentionally and oh-so-courageously was born as a human being and moved toward death on a cross. Talk about leaving one's comfort zone.

But this is our God—the God of ultimate risk; the God who assumes *seemingly* reckless action; the God who sends His infant Son into occupied territory, among an oppressed people; the God who entrusts His child to a virgin's womb; the God who enters humanity in the vulnerability of a newborn.

I think it is *safe* to say God is not the God of safeness. I recall the words of C. S. Lewis's Narnian when describing the great lion Aslan: "Safe? ... Who said anything about safe? 'Course he isn't safe. But he's good. He's the King, I tell you."[3]

God is most definitely not the God of the comfort zone.

God blows our self-protectionism apart. He calls upon those cowering among the baggage (like Saul), hiding in a winepress (like Gideon), retreating to the backside of the desert (like Moses). He uses the weak, the insufficient, and the inadequate. He takes away our safety nets, our self-insulation, our best-laid plans, and calls us out into the deep. But He has never challenged us with something He was not willing to first do Himself.

He consistently lays His all on the line. He set aside His divine privileges as Son of the Highest to subject Himself to servanthood and risk the hazards of a human body, not the least of which is death. Time and again, He narrowly escapes the perils of death, starting from the womb and not stopping until He lays His life down of His own free will.

This is our God. Sacrifice replaces safety. Courage displaces comfort. And danger does not deter.

But could you imagine if Jesus had never left heaven? If He had just cloistered Himself away, enjoying that safe, secure place with His Father? Because that's what we do. We play life safe. We live in safe neighborhoods. We send our kids to safe schools. We take safe vacations. We drive safe vehicles. We eat safe foods. We have safe friends.

Safety first.

What if "safety first" had been Jesus's modus operandi? What if He had decided to just "play it safe" and not ... leave ... heaven? Can you imagine? It's like one of those movies where someone is thrust back into the past to relive their story following a different course of events. What if Jesus had never come? Think of it!

No light. No hope. No love. No peace. No joy.

"Just blow out the Advent candles, folks. They're all gone. We're pressing rewind and heading back into the darkness." Can you grasp our fate had Jesus not come? Until He came and conquered sin, death, and hell, we had no hope of God's salvation. No hope of heaven. Thank God Jesus left! And not only did Jesus leave the safety of heaven, He went to the most notoriously dangerous place on earth.

The Middle East. Israel. Jerusalem.

The epicenter of a political and spiritual hotbed. You *still* can't pay some people enough to go there! And once He arrived, did He hide Himself away in the back forty, away from those who threatened His life? No. He was always in the open, right where the people were—the marketplace, the street, the temple, the roadway, the shore. He met His destiny arms wide open.

He risked it all when He left heaven. He *gave* all, so He could *save* all who receive Him. It was never about safety first. It was about His Father's plan—first. It was about you and me—first.

Is *He* my first? Or do I just float through life taking Him completely for granted? Taking for granted exactly how far

D

    O

        W

           N

                He came.

Down, He descended, lower than angels, from the form of God to the form of a human.

And not just any human, but a baby—the most vulnerable kind of a human there is.

> Then, the Son of God became a servant.
>
>> He didn't just humble Himself to the *life* of a human; He humbled Himself to our *death*.
>>
>>> And just to extend this some more, He didn't die as an old man, lying in his own bed, surrounded by his loving family as he slipped peacefully away in his sleep. Jesus was cut down in the prime of His youth, under horrifying circumstances, in the midst of those who hated Him, and strung up in broad daylight for every passing mocker to spit upon.
>>>
>>>> And I haven't even touched on the hell He plunged to in bearing away your sins and mine.
>>>>
>>>>> Could He get any lower?

Each Christmas, in our mind's eye, as we peer into the face of that babe of Bethlehem, the thought that He came so low should entirely shock us and completely humble our hearts.

Thankfully, the passage we began with doesn't end there, with the cross. There's a comma you might have missed, because it continues with these words:

> Therefore God has highly exalted him and bestowed on him the name that is above every name, so that at the name of Jesus every knee should bow, in

heaven and on earth and under the earth, and every tongue confess that Jesus Christ is Lord, to the glory of God the Father. (Philippians 2:9–11 ESV)

My friends, as we move deeper into this Christmas season and as we step further into His Light, His Hope, His Love, His Peace, His Joy, may we

> grow smaller,
>
> bend lower,
>
> come last …

so that He may grow *greater*, rise *higher*, and come *first*.

As John so aptly puts it, "He must increase, but I must decrease" (John 3:30 ESV).

> And so, Lord Jesus Christ, we lift You high!
> Mild he lays his glory by,
> Born that man no more may die,
> Born to raise the sons of earth,
> Born to give them second birth.

DAY 8

Fear Not

> And an angel of the Lord appeared to them, and the glory of the Lord shone around them, and they were filled with great fear. And the angel said to them, "Fear not, for behold, I bring you good news of great joy that will be to all people."
> —Luke 2:9–10 (ESV)

When I was a little girl, I used to think it would be so incredible to have an angel appear to me in my bedroom at night, just as they used to appear to people in the Bible. But I soon discovered most of those Bible heroes were extremely terrified at the appearance of an angel. In fact, the first words angels usually had to speak were "Fear not! Do not be afraid!" The more I imagined it, the more I decided it would be much too frightening to be startled by an angel, so I told God that on second thought, I had changed my mind; I was good.

These shepherds though ... I am certain they never ever forgot that night the angel came, accompanied by the glory of the Lord and then a host of others praising God! Weighing it all up, I'm sure they still would have said the heart attack was worth it! Can you imagine it? It's cold. It's a winter's night. You can see your breath. You're sitting around a fire to stay warm. Some of you sleep in shifts. You happen to be on duty, but slumber calls. Zzz …

Suddenly, the dark sky bursts into daylight! You cry out in horror! You've heard enough ghost stories in your time. Everyone's awake now! Even the sheep! Absolute terror! Panic reigns! Adrenaline is screaming through your body. You have no idea what is going on—is it fight? Is it flight? You hear the angel command you, "Fear not," but your mind is struggling hard to work out that you're being addressed by an angel! Then you're grasping to process the message—"good news … joy … a Savior … Messiah … a baby"—a baby? You hardly know whether to believe what you're hearing. Your mind is still numb from the collision of sleep and shock. You just about think you've understood the message and regained your cool when the heavens blast open yet again with now an army choir of heavenly hosts raising the sky with their praise, "Glory to God in the highest!" You're convinced you see your heart leave your body.

Then, almost as suddenly as they arrive, they're gone. You look around to see if any of your friends made it out alive. Did old Uncle Reuben pull through with that weak heart of his? You find young Cousin Jacob frozen with awe. You call out to each man, still dazzled by the wonder of it all. As shock dissipates, shouts of joy fill the air!

"Let's go! Let's check it out, men!"

"Let's see this amazing thing that has happened! What the Lord has made known to us!"

"Bethlehem?"

"Bethlehem!"

You leave it all behind: your sheep, your staff, your coat. You've never seen Uncle Reuben run so fast! The wind seems to carry you. You have no idea that what you are about to encounter is going to change your life … forever. You fly to the entrance of a cave, a sheep shelter, and then suddenly halt in your tracks, hearts pounding, lungs burning.

You know this place well. But never before have you witnessed here what you see now. A young man and woman beckon you forward. You slowly approach a crude feeding trough, a manger. You peer down at a child. Freshly born. Wrapped in swaddling clothes. Just as the angel said. You kneel with complete awe. Your rough hand instinctively reaches out, hesitates, and then touches ... the face of God. This is the Savior, Christ the Lord. You hear Uncle Reuben whisper, "Glory to God in the highest."

And as you worship, you realize it is true, that song of heaven. You murmur quietly, "Peace on earth, goodwill to men." And strangely you note—the fear is gone.

* * *

What would you give, my friend, to dispel the fear in your life? What would you pay for peace? What would you exchange for some good news of great joy?

The story of Christ's coming into the world was one of fear dispelled by hope. No less than four times do we hear the words of an angel, "Do not be afraid," only to follow with news of hope that results in joy.

We see an angel first arrive to Zechariah the priest, who would become the father of John the Baptist, the one to prepare the way for the Lord Jesus. When Zechariah first sees the angel, he is "gripped with fear," but the angel comforts him, "Do not be afraid" (Luke 1:11–13 NIV).

Then an angel appears to Mary, who is "greatly troubled" at the angel's greeting, so he assures her, "Do not be afraid" (Luke 1:28–30 NIV).

Next, an angel appears to Joseph in a dream and encourages him, "Do not be afraid" (Matthew 1:20 NIV).

Finally, an angel appears to the shepherds, and "they were terrified. But the angel said to them, 'Do not be afraid'" (Luke 2:9–10 NIV).

Not to fear is easier said than done. Let's face it; fear is a bully who charges into the room uninvited. And I know we've all been told faith overcomes fear, and fear cannot coexist with faith. How does the saying go? "Fear knocked at the door. Faith answered. There was no one there." But what happens when faith is faltering? What do you do when faith's wind has been knocked out of your sails? What if your faith isn't on hand to answer the door? What then?

It comes down to this truth—faith must always be based on something. Faith doesn't stand *alone*; it stands *upon*. And for a believer, that *something* is God's Word. What dispelled the fear for each of these characters? What brought these men and women the peace, hope, and courage to step forward in faith? Was it not the word of the Lord given to them by the angel? Was it not a word of truth from God Himself?

Zechariah was told the impossible—his barren wife would bear a son.

Mary was told the incredible—she would bear the Messiah.

Joseph was told the infallible—his wife was carrying *God's* Son.

The angels were told the inspirational—a Savior had been born.

Based on a word from the Lord, based on *truth*, each of these people were able to step past fear with faith. Faith doesn't just magically arrive. We can't stir it up on our own. We have no power within ourselves to flex faith. Faith is like the moon; it draws its light from the sun—and in our case, the Son. As we open God's Word, drink it in, and *believe* the truths *He* is speaking, the voice of fear shuts up and, in fact, is thrown from the room.

Did their circumstances change? For some of them, yes, things changed. Zechariah and Mary had sons. The angels found the Savior. But Joseph? Nothing about his immediate situation changed. When he awoke, his fiancée was still pregnant with a child not his own. The thing he had previously feared was still his reality, but the revelation of God's word and truth had in fact changed everything for him. God had assured him of His presence, His plan, and His peace in the situation, which gave Joseph the courage to move ahead.

Into what life circumstance do you need the command "Fear not" spoken? Over what waves do you need to hear "Do not be afraid"? Into which room has fear stepped, and from where does it need expelling? Go to God's Word; receive there His truth, His peace, His rest, His hope; and discover His "perfect love" that "casts out fear" (1 John 4:18 NKJV).

> "Fear not!" said he, for mighty dread
> Had seized their troubled mind.
> "Glad tidings of great joy I bring,
> To you and all mankind."

DAY 9

Show Me Your Glory

> And she gave birth to her firstborn son, and wrapped him in swaddling cloths and laid him in a manger … And suddenly there was with the angel a multitude of the heavenly hosts praising God and saying, 'Glory to God in the highest!'"
> (Luke 2:7, 13–14 ESV)

The Nativity was gritty.

A far fetch from the cozy Christmases we enjoy today. And perhaps you're like me. We love all the warm fuzzies of Christmastime—nestled in a chair with the flickering tree beside us, a crackling fire before us, snow falling beyond us through the window glass, carols playing softly around us. The Christmas season makes us come alive inside, despite the cold winds and icy roads. We love it all: the cheer, the gifts, the family time, and all the glitz and glam that dresses up our homes!

But the first Christmas was not glamorous at all. It wasn't the sanitized version we try to achieve in the here and now. We strive for the idyllic with our perfectly placed décor and never-ending cheery festivities. But the first Noel looked nothing like my white-washed willow tree crèche and nativity.

That night long ago was cold and dirty and agonizing. There was blood and straw and two teenagers ushering God into the world. Did they even know what they were doing? Had Mary seen birth before? Was Joseph the only one on hand to catch the Christ child? Were cattle the only outside witnesses to this moment? Was a starry sky the canopy under which Jesus came?

"Inglorious," you say.

And yet just a short distance off in the hills, one can hear the angelic choir raising the heavens with the strains of "Glory to God in the Highest …"

But where *is* the glory?

The Nativity doesn't sparkle. It doesn't glow. It doesn't shine.

It is rugged and raw and real. It is straw and sweat and soil.

So where is the glory?

Where is the awesome, majestic glory of which we must sing our praises to the highest? Where are the spectacular pillars of cloud and fire? Where is the glory that all kings of the earth tremble at? The consuming fire of God's greatness that terrified the Israelites, such that they feared they might die? So overwhelming, they could no longer bear it?

Where is the glory that Moses begged to be shown? The Shekinah that filled the tabernacle such that Moses could not enter? That permeated Solomon's temple such that the priests could not stand to minister? Where is the glory of God that sat between the cherubim? The glory that devoured the sacrifice?

Where is the glory that the heavens declare? Which heavenly beings ascribe to the Lord? Where is the power and glory David beheld in the sanctuary? God's excellence that manifested itself even in His judgment and thundered forth in His voice? Where is the glory that existed before the world began and endures forever?

Where is the smoke of Isaiah's day? The splendor set above

the heavens and exalted over the earth? Where is the gleaming brightness that brought Ezekiel to his face?

Where is the glory that by its very nature shouts all of God's radiance to all of heaven and all of earth? Filling all of time and all of eternity? The glory that blasts forth the excellencies of all His perfections, all His attributes, all His greatness, all His holy essence? Where is the majesty and the beauty of all that is God?

Where is the glory?

It's here.

In the dirt. In the straw. In the sheep cave. *This* is where the glory of God is.

It's in the womb of a virgin, sealed away in secret. Condensed into conception. Hidden and concealed where no eye can see. *This* is where the glory of God is.

It is God breaking onto the human scene through the womb of a virgin. In just one breath, the glory of God slipped from womb to world in the tiny body of a human baby. *This* is where the glory of God is.

It is God manifesting Himself to us in the skin of humanity and the face of an infant child. *This* is where the glory of God is.

And for a moment ... heaven is silent. Hushed in awe.

The great tabernacle of Moses's day? No. The ark of God and the cherubim of David's day? No. The magnificent temple of Solomon's day? No.

Where is the glory?

It's in the face of a newborn babe. "For God, who said, 'Let light shine out of darkness,' has shone in our hearts to give the light of the knowledge of the glory of God in the face of Jesus Christ" (2 Corinthians 4:6 ESV).

It's packaged in flesh and blood. "And the Word became flesh and dwelt among us, and we have seen his glory, glory as of the only Son from the Father, full of grace and truth" (John 1:14 ESV).

It's come to us in God's Son. "He is the radiance of the glory of God and the exact imprint of his nature, and he upholds the universe by the word of his power" (Hebrews 1:3 ESV).

This is where the glory of God is.

Who knew the countenance of God and all His glory would make its appearance to us in the face of a newborn? Who knew that humanity's first look into the face of God would have us peering into the face of a child? "Great is the mystery of godliness: God was manifested in the flesh" (1 Timothy 3:16 NKJV).

And heaven's silence breaks. The skies resound with the voice of the angel choir:

"Glory to God in the highest!"

Like Moses, we ask, "Show me your glory." And with the next breath, we realize God sent us His Son.

> Silent night, holy night
> Son of God, love's pure light
> Radiant beams from Thy holy face
> With the dawn of redeeming grace
> Jesus, Lord at Thy birth
> Jesus, Lord at Thy birth

10
DAY

God's Interruptions

And suddenly there was with the angel a multitude of the heavenly hosts praising God and saying, "Glory to God in the highest, and on earth peace among those with whom he is pleased!"
—Luke 2:13–14 (ESV)

I love how God just shows up.

Unexpected. Uninvited. Unexcused.

Suddenly, He's just there.

Abraham's going about his business in Ur, living the life he always knew, when suddenly God shows up and tells him to leave it all behind and "Go ... to the land that I will show you" (Genesis 12:1, ESV). You mean, pack up eighty years of life and head out into an unknown future?

Moses is herding a bunch of sheep in the backside of a desert when God shows up, and he meets the great I AM at the burning bush. "What are you doing out here, Moses? Go and free God's people."

"But I can't ... I'm not ... what if ... isn't there someone else?"

Then there's David—forgotten, insignificant, overlooked—tending his father's flock in the fields. God shows up, telling Samuel to anoint him as king. You'll be leading another flock, David—God's people, Israel.

Mary's going about her daily life when God shows up. "You will 'bear a son, and you shall call His name Jesus'" (Luke 1:31 ESV). But this could get complicated.

The shepherds are just logging in another long, cold night's work with the sheep, hoping Missy doesn't wander off and Petey doesn't roll on his back again. Suddenly, God shows up. "Unto you is born this day ... a Savior" (Luke 2:11 ESV). But they are just lowly shepherds. Why entrust them with this message?

Paul is on his way to destroy the church in Damascus when God shows up. Suddenly a great light from heaven shines around him. "Paul, you will share the gospel of Jesus to the Gentiles." Game-changer.

God doesn't always send a memo on ahead, like the school might do to warn of a practice fire drill. There are times when God *is* the memo. And He loves to show up precisely when you least expect it—in the humdrum of life, when you're on autopilot, when your mind is elsewhere, suddenly!

He doesn't always give you a heads-up, but instead He lifts up your head as though to say, "Pay attention. Something's about to change." And He doesn't ever have to apologize. His interruptions are what bless your life.

I admit I'm not really that good with interruptions. I don't like to pause the movie, put the book down, or stop the song midplay. When I'm in a groove, I don't like to break focus. My husband calls it "locked in." That said, kids have pretty much beaten the resistance out of me, but in an ideal world, could I please just finish my coffee first? (Ironically, of all the reflections I have written to date, this one was by far the most interrupted of them all! Not excluding a trip to the ER for a kid's fractured ankle!)

Not only do I not like interruptions, I am also hesitant to be the one interrupting. It took a lot of courage for me to agree to interrupting people's newsfeeds for twenty-five days straight when I first released this series of reflections!

But God doesn't feel awkward at all about interrupting our lives. Aside from the fact He has every authority to do so, He knows that His interruptions are going to break us out of the deep set of tracks we are set in to move us in a better direction—His direction. He's going to trouble our waters to extend the ripples of impact—His impact. He's going to take our neat and tidy little plans and throw us into the midst of a greater plan—His plan. So no, He doesn't feel badly nor is He sorry for interrupting our lives. It's we who need to get comfy with it.

The only thing you can expect is ... the unexpected.

And the last thing the people of Jesus's day expected was Him.

So what kind of Messiah were they expecting? What did they think they needed to change their world? Given the Roman rule they were under, I would think they were hoping for a military leader, a zealous warrior, perhaps, to at last conquer their foes and deliver them to freedom. Maybe they expected a mighty king in the vein of the great king David.

In tracing over their prophets' writings and even in listening to Mary's Magnificat and Zechariah's prophecy following the birth of his son, John the Baptist, one can learn much about what the Jews were anticipating in their coming Messiah. And if they had really paid close attention to the prophecies, they should have seen it coming. They should have seen *Him* coming, but they didn't. And I can tell you one thing ...

Nobody anticipated Jesus.

Nobody looked for the offspring of a "questionable" woman and her penniless fiancé from the no-good town of Nazareth. (I speak now as an onlooker of that day with the exception of the godly few.) "Is not this the carpenter's son?" they would scoff (Matthew 13:55 ESV). "Can anything good come out of Nazareth?" they would ask (John 1:46 ESV).

Nobody awaited a kingdom that blessed the poor in spirit or those who mourn or the meek and those hungry for righteousness or the merciful and the pure in heart or the peacemakers and the persecuted. No. Nobody bargained for any of this.

No one foresaw a manger throne or royal swaddling cloths or an eventual crown of thorns. Not even close.

With the glory days of David and Solomon long since over and centuries of being passed from one master's hand to another, the nation longed for the restoration of a bygone era. But the waiting had worn them down, and so they had slipped into the rut of routine and religion …

When suddenly, God showed up.

In the person of Jesus Christ.

When they least expected it, how they least envisioned it, and whom they least awaited. It's really sad they weren't anticipating the Messiah in the person of Jesus.

What are you expecting this Christmas season? Some happy times with those in your family? A few board games, perhaps? Maybe a carol sing? A turkey dinner? A sleigh ride or a few runs to the ski hill? Snowmobiling, tubing, skating? Maybe that gift you've been wanting? Cozy times opening stockings and presents?

What are you expecting out of … life?

Are you hoping for Jesus? Are you awaiting His coming? When He arrives, will you be surprised or disappointed?

May I encourage you to watch for Him this season? Anticipate His coming. Wait for Him this year.

So that when He does show up, you will be expecting Him.

> Joy to the world! The Lord has come
> Let earth receive her King!
> Let every heart prepare Him room
> And heaven and nature sing

11

DAY

The Gift-Wrapped Lamb

> And this will be a sign for you: you will find a baby wrapped in swaddling cloths and lying in a manger.
> —Luke 2:12 (ESV)

Gift-wrapping is one of those ventures that can tell a whole story.

I'm pretty sure you could profile a person based on their gift-wrapping abilities. There's the perfectionist, like my hubby, who may or may not measure the paper before cutting (measure twice, cut once), who painstakingly ensures his perfect ninety-degree folds, who probably even has a standardized length of tape strip he uses (eye roll). His gifts are something to behold, let me tell ya. Flawless. I could get jealous, but I just remind myself that I wrap about 350 billion presents to the two he wraps for me. So, there's always that (shrug).

Then there are those Martha Stewart types who show up right about now on social media, just to expose the inadequacies of the rest of us 99 percent, with all their gorgeously packaged, creatively trimmed, and stunningly arranged parcels. (Thank goodness my kids don't judge me by my wrapping work). But seriously, I really do love oohing and awing over the eye-candy these girls post for us.

I think, though, my favorite kind of wrapped gifts are the ones that look like they fell out of a plane into a war zone and then got shipped around the world about three times before being dragged through the snow by a pack of ravening wolves, only to be rescued by an adorable, brave-hearted five-year-old little girl, who hands me the most-definitely homemade gift, packaged in the most-definitely homemade wrapping paper. Sigh. I'm mush.

Contents of the gift aside, packaging can tell a whole story.

I've often wondered why Mary chose to package baby Jesus in swaddling cloths. Was it all she could afford because of her poverty? (No trimmed-out million-dollar nursery here.) Or maybe cotton cloth was all she had on hand because they were travelling? (Ever the pragmatist?) Or, then again, was swaddling cloth simply the typical way to wrap a child born at this time? Hmmm.

I did some digging and learned some fascinating facts about swaddling cloth. I discovered it was not by random accident, of course. They were typical and yet profound. So like God to layer something extraordinary into something that is actually completely ordinary. It was indeed traditional practice for Jewish mothers to wash their infants, salt them to ward off infection, and finally swaddle them in long strips of cotton swaddling bands to replicate the tightness of the womb (Ezekiel 16:4).

But more intriguing is the fact that this was given as a sign to the shepherds who came to visit the Christ. The angel had said, "And this will be a sign for you: you will find a baby wrapped in swaddling cloths and lying in a manger" (Luke 2:12 ESV).

According to certain Jewish scholars, the shepherds of the nativity were not just any shepherds. They were Levitical shepherds in charge of the lambs raised for sacrifices. When the time came for these lambs to be born, the sheep were brought into the shepherds' caves, where they would give birth. The baby lambs were then swaddled in linen cloths so as to keep them spotless and without blemish for sacrifice.

So when these shepherds, who were raising these lambs for temple sacrifices, saw the baby Messiah wrapped in swaddling cloths, born in the same place as the Passover lambs, the significance that this was God's Passover Lamb who would take away the sin of the world would not have been lost on them.

Amazing.

There in a stone manger, not a far cry from an altar, lay the little Lamb of God, wrapped in the cloths of a sacrificial lamb.

I am reminded of Isaac's question so many thousands of years before: "Behold, the fire and the wood, but where is the lamb for a burnt offering?" (Genesis 22:7 ESV). To which, Abraham replies, "God will provide for himself the lamb for a burnt offering" (Genesis 22:8 ESV). And here we are in Bethlehem centuries later, and we see God's provision—a Lamb set apart for sacrifice. Himself.

Yes, He would be set apart, just like all Passover Lambs were, to be observed for any spots and blemishes—not because God wondered if He might have any, but to demonstrate to us that this Lamb was, in fact, perfect. But Jesus Christ would not be observed for a mere four days, like all the other Passover lambs. No, He would go on to live for thirty-three years under the scrutiny of both God and man.

Such was the sinless perfection of Christ that the apostle Peter, who walked as one of those closest to Christ and witnessed His life, words, and actions, concluded Jesus Christ to be "a lamb without blemish or spot" (1 Peter 1:19 ESV). Peter goes on to record, "He committed no sin, neither was deceit found in his mouth" (1 Peter 2:22 ESV). The great apostle Paul also agreed that He "knew no sin" (2 Corinthians 5:21 ESV). And yet another close disciple and apostle, John, attested that "in him there is no sin" (1 John 3:5 ESV).

Therefore, the Son of God, pure and sinless in every possible way, was able to be "the Lamb of God, who takes away the sin of the world!" (John 1:29 ESV).

Oh, I know, we don't like to talk of such somber things at Christmastime. But was it not because of the Lamb provided that we even have occasion to celebrate anything? Is He not the cause of the joy we share this season? Is He not the source of all our peace and light during Christmas and besides? And is the Lamb not the One who gives us entrance into our ultimate hope of heaven?

Why yes, it is only because our names are written in the Lamb's book of life that we will enjoy heaven (Revelation 13:8, 21:27). It is only because we are the bride of Christ that we will enter into the marriage supper of the Lamb (Revelation 19:7–9, 21:9). And it is only because of the Lamb that we will enjoy His emanating light in that beautiful place (Revelation 21:23). There is no heaven without the Lamb, and it is to the Lamb that our praises will sound for all eternity. This, my friends, is why the Lamb must indeed be referenced at Christmastime.

It's perfectly fine to enjoy our cozy, Christmassy homes. It's completely okay to snuggle up by our fireplaces, sip our eggnog, and listen to our favorite carols. And it's absolutely all right to admire our trees, delight in our décor, and anticipate our presents.

But never lose sight of the Lamb. Place Him in a prominent place in your heart and on your hearth.

> Because   heaven.
>   heaven   up to
>   came   us
>   down   bring
>   to us   could
>   as a Lamb, so that the Lamb

> Mary did you know?
> Did you know that your baby boy
> Is Heaven's perfect Lamb?
> The sleeping child you're holding
> Is the great I AM

12
DAY

In Search of the King

> Where is he who has been born king of the Jews? For we have seen his star when it rose and have come to worship him.
> —Matthew 2:2 (ESV)

It was embarrassing.

An envoy of eastern magi stood before King Herod, asking him if *he* knew where the new King was. He hadn't a clue! Hadn't heard of *any* king of any kind laying claim to his throne, least of all a Jewish baby! As preposterous as it was, the news disturbed him deeply—and all Jerusalem with him. It troubled the court, and their distressed whispers poured out into the streets.

Herod's Jewish scholars flew into action, digging through the ancient scrolls on threat of Herod's anger, to find the location of the Messiah's birth—Bethlehem. It was equally upsetting how up to this point these foreign magi seemed to know more about the Messiah's coming than Herod's leading priests and teachers of religious law. Herod's secure world was rocked to the core.

But really, it shouldn't have come as any surprise that the magi were so well-versed in ancient Scripture. Most certainly, Daniel's high position centuries before in the Babylonian courts and his influence in their universities had endured. These magi would have known his prophecy concerning the coming of an "anointed one" (Daniel 9:26 ESV).

Indeed, two of their very own kings had declared that God's kingdom would last forever and His rule would never end (Daniel 4:3, 34, 6:26). They also had Daniel's detailed time line of events and apparently had been waiting expectantly for the arrival of this King of the Jews.

Furthermore, it is quite possible these wise men were familiar with the prophecy that "A star shall come out of Jacob, and a scepter shall rise out of Israel" (Numbers 24:17 ESV). As intelligent students of the sky, they were able to recognize Christ's star when it appeared. And they rejoiced at what it signaled—the birth of the King of the Jews. It is this truth, divinely revealed through God's Word and supported with a sign that launched these men on their journey in search of the King.

So here they stood before Herod. Yet for all their wisdom and knowledge, bless their beautiful hearts, I'm not sure if these precious magi fully understood what they had stirred up in Jerusalem—that is, until later when God warned them in a dream not to go back to Herod and told them to return home by another way (Matthew 2:12).

For them, the birth of the King of the Jews was cause for celebration. It had never occurred to them that the news might mean anything but joy. When they "saw the star, they rejoiced exceedingly with great joy" (Matthew 2:10 ESV). But they had yet to learn that the King always evokes a division in response—delight or dismay, worship or woe, acceptance or rejection.

And so, they had arrived at Jerusalem fully expecting this King to be where He should be—in the royal palace. And no one should fault them for this assumption. Sadly, the King wasn't there. Were they disappointed? Maybe. Had the search let them down? A little. Did they turn back for home? Certainly not!

No, wise men are never satisfied until they *find* the King. And so, they moved forward with new truth that He was to be born in Bethlehem, they caught a new vision of His star, and they did find Him with great joy!

I am challenged by their single-minded search for the King. Somehow, these wise men knew the journey could only culminate at Christ. The destination must always be the King. *He* is the quest. How often do I wander in my search? Chasing butterflies? Chasing the wind? Pursuing a destiny other than Him?

How often do I pursue the gifts but not the Giver? The crowns but not the King? The goods but not my God? The stuff but not the Son? The quest but not the Christ? All of the things but the King of kings?

I don't want to go through this season or, in fact, go through life missing Him! To one day, in all my pursuing and striving and grasping and desiring, look around and discover I've arrived at the wrong destination. To realize I've missed Him completely. I've missed the Giver, the God, the King, the Son, the Christ.

Herod kept missing the King. Oh, he tried to find Him! Desperately he sought for the child but was never able to find Him. The baby always eluded his grasp, forever escaped his clutches, and entirely evaded his discovery. Herod tore a path of violent destruction in search of the Christ—to seek and destroy. But he never found the King.

The wise men do though.

Wise men *always* find the King.

They find Him because they are searching for Him as their King. Are you searching for the King? Have you found Him? In all the clatter of Christmas and all the glitter of gifts or in all the despair of darkness—whatever your distractions might be—are you searching for the King?

If you're having difficulty in this season, might I suggest

looking up to heaven for His star? Lift your eyes from your life's circumstances to gaze up at the One who is "the bright and morning Star" (Revelation 22:16).

Because if you find the star … you find the King.

> And by the light of that same star
> The wise men came from country far
> To seek for a king was their intent
> And to follow the star wherever it went
> Noel, Noel, Noel, Noel
> Born is the King of Israel

DAY 13

The Greatest Gift

She will bear a son, and you shall call his name Jesus, for he will save his people from their sins.
—Matthew 1:21 (ESV)

For unto you is born this day in the city of David a Savior, who is Christ the Lord.
—Luke 2:11 (ESV)

What if all you got for Christmas this year was *Jesus*?

What if He were your only company? What if you couldn't gather with family? What if there were no friends, no grandma and grandpa, no uncles and aunts, no cousins, no big turkey dinner? What if the only one sitting at your table with you this year was Jesus?

Would you be okay with that? Would you be happy with His companionship? Just you and Jesus. No one else. Nothing else. Would that be your idea of a wonderful yuletide celebration? A Christmas for the books?

What if there were no great pile of presents to unwrap? No gifts under the tree from loved ones? What if Jesus were your only gift?

What if your only gift this Christmas was the present of His presence?

Would you be satisfied?

My children are struggling this year with not being able to see their cousins. On more than one occasion, my oldest son has sighed and said, "Mom, I would trade all my gifts this year just to be with my cousins." Not once has he begged me for a present. More than once, he has begged me for their presence.

What would I be willing to trade for the gift of His presence? What is the gift of *Jesus* worth to me? As the very meaning of His name implies, Jesus is the source of our salvation, our Savior. But how much do I value Jesus my Savior?

The gift of Jesus was rejected by the people of His day, His own people. They were looking for a savior to rescue them from Roman rule. They had seen the miracles Jesus had done and wondered if He might be the one to save them ... from their Roman overlords. In fact, just one week before His death, as Jesus rode into Jerusalem on a donkey, the people cried out, "Hosanna! Hosanna!" meaning, "Save us, we pray! Save us, we pray!" They were ready to crown Him as the king and savior of their imagining, of how they saw fit that He should rule.

So, what went sideways? How did they go from nearly crowning Him one week to crucifying Him the next? It became evident to them that He wasn't the savior they were looking for after all. His goal was not to save His people from the mastery of the Romans (though His redemption will eventually destroy all evil forms of mastery). His purpose was to save His people from the mastery of their sins, which was the very plan put forth in the name given to Him at His birth: "And you shall call his name Jesus, for he will save his people from their sins" (Matthew 1:12 ESV).

But they rejected Him as their Savior. They turned their backs on the only means of God's salvation for them. Jesus was not the savior they wanted, although He was the Savior they most desperately needed. They misunderstood that there is no salvation from the effects of sin without there being salvation from the cause of sin. Peter and John later counter the Jews' rejection of Jesus, saying, "There is salvation in no one else, for there is *no other name* under heaven given among men by which we must be saved" (Acts 4:12 ESV, my emphasis added). No other name than *Jesus*.

Today's crowd is no different. It still sets Jesus aside. There He sits, the unopened gift. Unreceived, unbelieved, unwelcomed. And sadly, people miss out on the greatest gift. But that gift is still available today to all who believe on His name (John 1:14). The offer still stands; Jesus still awaits receiving. And "If you confess with your mouth that Jesus is Lord and believe in your heart that God raised him from the dead, you will be saved" (Romans 10:9 ESV).

And for those of us who have believed on His name and have received the gift of the Savior, do we still enjoy Him? Do we daily seek Jesus? Or do we step past Him on our way out the door? I am challenged at the memory of those devoted Greeks who asked, "Sir, we wish to see Jesus" (John 12:21 ESV).

Furthermore, do I understand all that my Savior is? Because the story of Jesus doesn't end with His saving death and resurrection, incredible as that is. Luke adds something in his gospel record that takes our joy to the next level. Listen to the promise given to Mary by the angel of the Lord:

"And behold, you will conceive in your womb and bear a son, and you shall call his name Jesus. He will be great and will be called the Son of the Most High. And the Lord God will give to him the throne of his father David, and he will reign over the house of Jacob forever, and of his kingdom there will be no end" (Luke 1:31–33 ESV).

No wonder Mary exclaims, "My spirit rejoices in God my Savior" (Luke 1:47 ESV). This Savior will be great! Yes, this very same Jesus who had to subject Himself to the suffering of the cross will be great! Not only called Jesus but also called the Son of the Most High, exulted to an eternal throne of an everlasting kingdom—*Jesus,* who was brought so low, will be raised so high!

Never undervalue the name of *Jesus.* The rights to the throne and all the glory and titles that He wears come by way of *Jesus's* death on the cross. It is as *Jesus* that He won the renown. And it is precisely because of *Jesus's* work of salvation that Paul writes,

> Therefore God has highly exalted him and bestowed on him the name that is above every name, so that at the name of Jesus every knee should bow, in heaven and on earth and under the earth, and every tongue confess that Jesus Christ is Lord, to the glory of God the Father. (Philippians 2:9–11 ESV)

Jesus. Name above all names. It is the name to which all things will one day bow!

But maybe we are a little like the disciples this season. They ascended onto a mountain with Jesus and became distracted with others who took away from their singular focus on *Jesus.* God stripped away all that hindered their view. And perhaps this year, God is doing the same with us—stripping away all our distractions so that we too will gain a clearer vision of *Jesus* alone. We are told that "when they lifted their eyes, they saw no one but Jesus only" (Matthew 17:8 ESV).

What do we need to lift our eyes from?

Our circumstances? The world out there? The waves around us? The things taken from us this year? The stresses and pressures calling our names? Or maybe the good and grand things? Maybe the impressive that seeks to steal the limelight from Jesus? Who or what is competing with Jesus for your attention right now?

Lift your eyes, friend.

Lift them to His cradle—"But we see Jesus, who was made a little lower than the angels."

Lift them to His cross—"For the suffering of death."

Lift them to His crown—"Crowned with glory and honor" (Hebrews 2:9 NKJV).

And unwrap the Greatest Gift—*Jesus*.

"Thanks be to God for His indescribable gift!" (2 Corinthians 9:15 NKJV).

> How silently, how silently
> The wondrous gift is given
> So God imparts to human hearts
> The blessings of His Heaven
> No ear may hear His coming
> But in this world of sin
> Where meek souls will receive Him still
> The dear Christ enters in

14

DAY

Fall on Your Knees

> And going into the house, they saw the child with Mary
> his mother, and they fell down and worshipped him.
> —Matthew 2:11 (ESV)

This is not the posture of kings.

To fall down before a child?

What so moved these royals that they would abandon decorum and propriety in this way? Surely this was not customary, especially considering the child's humble circumstances. These kings of the east exuded wealth and power and dignity. They were at home in royal courts, accustomed to holding audiences with kings of similar pedigree. Had they not just come from Herod's palace? They were intelligent, astute, and well-versed in ancient Scripture and prophecy. They had the means to fund a many-months-long search for a royal child.

(Retellings of the nativity often mistakenly place the kings at the stable, when in fact, Christ's birth and star is what launched them on their quest. By the time the kings arrived to visit the child,

Joseph and Mary had already moved into a house, and Jesus would have likely been between one and two years of age).

Imagine though, the striking contrast when this wealthy envoy of kings rolled up in front of Joseph and Mary's humble house, a group of well-attired men riding well-groomed camels, bearing gifts of great worth, their foreign robes made of rich fabrics and vibrant colors, with servants in attendance.

Quite the opposite to the lowly abode in front of them. Joseph would have done the home proud as a carpenter, of course, but as they were poor, the structure would have been simple. Whitewashed stone walls, no doubt. Classic flat roof with beams running lengthwise and thick straw mats padded down. No fancy furniture or decor. Just the necessary stools, pots, jars, hearth. Herbs hanging from the ceiling beams perhaps. Humble but homey.

I imagine Joseph would have been surprised by the arrival of these kings, maybe taken a little off guard, unsure of what to make of it. Yet his small family had gone through so many other marvels in their short history with little Jesus, I'm sure he recovered quickly enough to welcome them in. What guests, really! To host kings! What an honor! And yet, he would have known whom they were really looking for.

The kings too might have been somewhat surprised at their terminus. After all, their first stop had been Herod's palace, a far more suitable home for a king. This humble home was not what they were expecting, but it was to this place the star had led them and come to rest (Matthew 2:9).

The kings are granted entrance into the small house. They are full of great expectation—to at long last find what their search has brought them to. And there He is. They see Him. The Child. With his mother, Mary. Was she holding Him as she worked by the hearth? Was He sitting on her lap as she fed him? Was He hugging her leg as she greeted the kings? What matters is they saw Him!

Can you envision it? A lowly child holding court in the closed-in, dirt-floored living quarters of an ordinary home in Bethlehem's poor district for representatives of earth's highest houses. Instantly, these grown men, these polished kings, fall down and worship Him, recognizing in this small child a greater King! They no longer see the stone walls, dirt floor, or even the child's mother. They see only one thing before them—the eternal King of heaven robed in human flesh—and they know themselves to be in the presence of the King of kings and Lord of lords (Revelation 19:16, 17:14).

This scene is familiar to us. Where have we seen it before? Somewhere buried in Scripture. In an almost déjà-vu-like fashion, we know this sight of earthly kings bowing to this One who is born King, this One who in His essential person is worthy of kingship from His very birth.

We are taken to Isaiah's prophecy, some seven hundred years preceding this event, in which he foretells, "Nations shall come to your light, and kings to the brightness of your rising" (Isaiah 60:3 ESV). Yes, yes, these kings have come to His light, but where have we seen them bowing before the King? Oh, it's Isaiah again, also telling us, "Kings shall see and arise; princes, and they shall prostrate themselves ... With their faces to the ground they shall bow to you" (Isaiah 49:7, 23 ESV). That's right. It is in Isaiah's writings and others like his that we have witnessed this very scene.

And yet, this moment of kings bowing before the child King—with all of its unimaginable wonder and awe and pure joy—is just a microcosm, a mere foretaste of a moment still to come, prophetic of a greater moment still awaiting us. Or in the spirit of technicalities, it is one of two phases in Isaiah's prophecy, having a fulfillment in the near future and a fulfillment in the distant future.

These few representative Gentile kings bowing before the child King give us a glimpse into the final phase of Isaiah's prophecy concerning a future day, in which all nations will come to Christ's light and honor and worship the great King when He shall reign forever (Revelation 15:4, 21:24). It will be a glorious day when so much prophecy regarding the King will come to fruition. If this small scene touches your heart, just you wait!

"Your eyes will behold the king in his beauty; they will see a land that stretches afar" (Isaiah 33:17 ESV). And at long last, the Lord will set his king upon His holy hill of Zion (Psalm 2:6). Christ will no longer be the rejected King but will be the King recognized by the entire world. And His kingdom will be wonderful because He will reign in righteousness (Isaiah 32:1).

Yes, one day, this small interchange, upon the dusty dirt floor of a tiny Judean home, will come to life on a universal and eternal scale, with the kings of the earth bowing to "Jesus Christ ... the prince of the kings of the earth" (Revelation 1:5–6 KJV), the "King of the nations" (Revelation 15:3 ESV). This is the grand design projected forward from one brief, awe-filled moment in Bethlehem where, prostrate, a handful of kings worship the Christ child—their royal knees buckled beneath them, their pride and dignity bowed low. And with complete humility, they honor the One who is born King.

And suddenly I am there too, with them in the presence of the King.

Am I still standing? What's my posture? If earth's highest dignitaries bowed before Him, and royal kings all but crowned Him, who am I to remain standing?

Do I see only a child and not see the King? Do I see only a cradle and not see His crown? Do I see only a boy and not see His throne? Is my vision so tragically short-sighted?

Or have I been standing for so long, I've forgotten how to kneel?

Maybe it's time for me to swap my resistance for reverence, my hesitancy for humility, my words for worship, my doubts for devotion, my indecision for adoration, my delay for delight, my pause for praise.

Maybe it's time that I too bend low, fall before Him, and worship the eternal King of kings.

> Fall on your knees
> O hear the angels' voices
> O night divine
> O night when Christ was born

Day 15

Great Expectations

> But Mary treasured up all these things, pondering them in her heart … And his mother marveled at what was said about him … And Simeon … said to Mary … "(A sword will pierce through your own soul also)."
> —Luke 2:19, 33, 35 (ESV)

Mary treasured all these things.

Isn't this just what we mothers do?

Treasure all the things; love our babies, young and grown; and tuck the moments away in our hearts. And Mary was no different. She pondered it all as she watched grown men cry and earthly kings fall prostrate before the baby she bore. As she witnessed people interact with the Christ child, we are told she treasured all these things in her heart.

No doubt she was amazed by the events and in awe of the child. How many times did she stare at Him with wonder, reflect on all that was said of Him, and assess the responses He drew from people?

This is mother territory. We watch our children with amazement, long for them with hope for the future, love them with hearts burst wide open—open to it all, the joys and the sorrows. The treasures enrich us but lay us bare all at once.

When we first meet Mary, she is full of questions for the angel and has so much to say to her cousin Elizabeth. She is bubbling with excitement and enthusiasm for God's plan, bursting with joy and wonder in her Magnificat. But as she gets deeper into God's plan and as the great story of Christ's coming truly unfolds, Mary moves from many words to fewer and fewer, until at last she has nothing left to say at all, but instead she ponders these things in the secluded quiet space of her heart.

I wonder at which point Mary realized things weren't going according to how she envisioned.

When Jesus was a mere eight days old, the righteous and devout Simeon had told her, "A sword will pierce through your own soul also" (Luke 2:33 ESV). A sobering moment for sure. Not entirely as she expected and not exactly what she had signed up for.

There had already been some difficulties and some evidence that the way forward would not be easy. The news of her pregnancy had not been met entirely with belief but with scandal. Her fiancé had nearly divorced her. There was the awkward timing of the census that had forced them to travel while she was pregnant. There was the inconvenience of having no place to bear the child. And now this. A sword?

I don't think Mary for a moment doubted God's plan for her life, but I do think she wondered at times with how it was coming to pass. Mary was a godly girl, evident by her immediate and humble submission to God's will as His servant. It is clear she had a deep understanding of Scripture, as seen in her song of praise.

She valued the high honor bestowed upon her in bringing the Messiah into the world. And yet the journey forward had not been easy. It had not come without hardship and inconvenience. Whatever dreams she and Joseph had of white picket fences were set to one side as they started their family in an animal shelter and soon fled as refugees into Egypt.

The journey God calls us into is never guaranteed to rise to the level of worldly expectation. He calls us to surrender our safety and lay down our expectations, to flesh out our faith with trust. Faith reaches out to what is unseen, whereas, trust is built by what *is* seen.

I think Mary always had faith, but she needed to learn to trust. She had faith in the mission and faith in the God who told her so. But she had to learn to trust God in how He was working it out. And there is evidence that Mary did learn to trust. Years later at a wedding in Cana, when the wine ran out, she turned unhesitatingly to Jesus for help. Then, without missing a beat, she instructed the servants, "Whatever he says to you, do it" (John 2:5 NKJV). She fully knew that "whatever" could literally mean whatever! She had lived this out. But she had learned to trust that whatever that "whatever" was just to do it.

Maybe you're like Mary. You have all the faith in the world, but you're still learning to trust. You're afraid of the sword that might pierce your soul. You're afraid of the hard journey. You're afraid of dashed expectations. You're afraid that one day you may find yourself at the cross of your son. These are the things you are pondering in your heart—a mixture of hope in God's promises and fear in how He's bringing it to pass.

What would Mary say to you? What would Mary tell herself? Would she take you on that journey from the exuberant joy of knowing God was going to use her for something great to the heart-rending sorrow of standing beneath her crucified son? And then travel the whole road in between those two points?

I'm sure, year after year, she went back over the ground again and again and always somehow arrived right back at the very beginning, to the moment God first appeared to her and revealed His plan. I imagine she clung to that moment with all her might. The promises declared.

From there, she would've retraced the remaining thirty-three years and marked each moment when trust was built one brick at a time, bringing shape to the faith she first knew, faith giving way to sight, what was unseen becoming seen. I believe she would tell us to go back to our beginning, to that moment when God first revealed Himself to us. To go back to His promises from His Word. That's what Mary would tell us.

And how do I know that her faith and trust were not destroyed by the cross? Forty days after Jesus's death, you find her sitting in an upper room with all those who loved Him, waiting with faith and expectation for the promised Holy Spirit, who would come and fill each present heart (Acts 1:13–14, 2:1–4).

Friend, I don't know what your heart's treasures are. I don't know God's plan for your life. I don't know the sword you're fearing. I don't know the events you're pondering. But I think we can all take a page from Mary's book and listen to her trusted advice: "Whatever He says to you, do it" (John 2:5 NKJV) … whatever that "whatever" is.

> Mary did you know that your baby boy
> Would save our sons and daughters?
> Did you know that your baby boy
> Has come to make you new?
> This child that you delivered,
> Will soon deliver you

16

DAY

The Queen and Her King

> They saw the child ... and they fell down and worshipped him. Then, opening their treasures, they offered him gifts, gold and frankincense and myrrh.
> —Matthew 2:11 (ESV)

I love the layers of Scripture. Turning its pages is like extracting emeralds buried in silver, only to find diamonds layered with gold. It reads like a multifaceted poem and sings like the song of a symphony. No word out of place and few notes sounding alone.

The journey of the magi and the gifts they bring is no different—reminiscent of another royal voyage made thousands of years prior to Christ's birth.

She was called the Queen of Sheba.

And she had questions. Hard questions.

Oh, she had heard the stories. She had sifted through the

accounts, tales of an extravagant kingdom beyond imagination, legends of a king so magnificent in power and wealth it was past taking in. Yes, she had "heard of the fame of Solomon concerning the name of the Lord" (1 Kings 10:1 ESV). But she would not be contented just to hear of him. She would go and see him for herself.

So, like the magi of Jesus's day, who searched for the Prince of Peace, this queen traveled to see the king of peace, Solomon. Both envoys came from afar, both carried gold and spices, and both journeys ended in praise, awe, and worship.

When Isaiah foretells the visit of the kings to the Christ child, he actually draws upon Queen Sheba's historic visit to King Solomon:

> And nations shall come to your light, and kings to the brightness of your rising ... the wealth of the nations shall come to you. A multitude of camels shall cover you, the young camels of Midian and Ephah; all those from Sheba shall come. They shall bring gold and frankincense, and shall bring good news, the praises of the LORD. (Isaiah 60:3, 5–6 ESV)

Isaiah's prophetic parallel between the magi and the Queen of Sheba is profound. The queen too was drawn by the king. She had heard of Solomon's wisdom and fame, and it drew her in. Before her lay 1,500 miles of desert to traverse, which would have taken months. At one point, Jesus tells us, "she came from the ends of the earth" (Matthew 12:42 ESV). A great distance, to be sure. Similarly, the magi were drawn by Christ's light, which pulled them on their own long journey to the King. For them, the star was no mere call to adventure. It was a call to worship.

Like the magi, the queen arrives at Jerusalem in search of the king. She comes with a "great retinue, with camels bearing spices and very much gold and precious stones" (1 Kings 10:2 ESV). Clearly a woman of great wealth. The magi come equally prepared with rich gifts to honor the King, as prophesied by Isaiah.

And after all the grandeur, majesty, and wisdom she witnesses in King Solomon's court, the Queen of Sheba is left only with complete amazement and wonder. Such was the overwhelming splendor of what she saw, it is said that "there was no more breath in her" (1 Kings 10:5 ESV). In awe, she responds with praise and admiration, having only been told the half of what she was now seeing before her eyes:

> "Blessed be the Lord your God, who has delighted in you and set you on the throne of Israel! Because the Lord loved Israel forever, he has made you king, that you may execute justice and righteousness." Then she gave the king 120 talents of gold, and a very great quantity of spices and precious stones. Never again came such an abundance of spices as these that the queen of Sheba gave to King Solomon. (1 Kings 10:9–10 ESV)

The hopes of David for his son Solomon had come to pass in the Queen of Sheba's visit, as he expresses in his final psalm:

> May the kings of Sheba ... bring gifts! May all kings fall down before him, all nations serve him! ... May gold of Sheba be given to him! ... May his name endure forever, his fame continue as long as the sun! May people be blessed in him, all nations call him blessed! (Psalm 72:10–15, 17 ESV)

Unknowingly, David spoke not only of his son Solomon but of his greater Son, Jesus Christ.

The magi also fall down and worship before the Messiah, who is King. And they do present Him with gold and spices, following the example of the ancient Queen of Sheba. And like her, they too praise the King with great joy of heart and depart fully satisfied with all they discover in their King. It was said of the Queen of Sheba that the king gave to her "all that she desired, whatever she asked besides what was given to her by the bounty of the king" (1 Kings 10:13 ESV). And this is how she went away—with all her wonderings satisfied and then some!

This draws me into our own journey to the King. Yes, the journey seems long at times. We are certain of the destination but uncertain of the road between. And just as the Queen of Sheba "came to test him with hard questions" (1 Kings 10:1 ESV), there are days in our journey when we too bring hard questions before our King. And though it might seem impertinent of us to ask, like Solomon, our King is never dismayed or annoyed, but instead, He welcomes and assures us.

Perhaps, like the queen, you have a lot on your mind this season. There are things you wonder about and worry over. Hard things. Things that can't be held back. And like the Queen of Sheba, you carry these along in your journey as an unseen collection of concerns, your fears and your tears, to present before the King. Well, when she arrived, she held nothing back! "She told him all that was on her mind" (1 Kings 10:2 ESV).

And he did not disappoint: "Solomon answered all her questions; there was nothing hidden from the king that he could not explain to her" (1 Kings 10:3 ESV). Our King is "someone greater than Solomon" (Matthew 12:42 NLT). He is even more able to answer if you would only just follow the queen's example and lay it all out before Him.

But if hard questions were all the queen carried with her, there would be nothing for the king. His answers were his gift to her, but her treasures were her gift for him. And this is where some of us fall short. Maybe we do bring our questions to Christ. Maybe we do lay it all before Him and tell Him all that is on our mind. But then we get up and walk away, leaving nothing for Him, nothing for the King.

Not this queen. Besides her hard questions, she also brought rich gifts for the king. And like her, the magi also carried with them their treasures for the King. The gifts of gold, frankincense, and myrrh. The gold measuring His worth. The frankincense referencing His priestly walk. The myrrh foreshadowing His work as the sacrificial Lamb of God. The magi knew the value of the King. He was not One just to be plundered for wisdom but also One to be pondered with worship.

What gifts do you have for the King this season? Do you have anything to lay at His feet? Of your time, service, talents, love, affection, or praise? Are there any treasures at all within that heart of yours? He deserves your best! Lay them all down before Him, hold nothing back, and present them to your King!

> Born a king on Bethlehem's plain
> Gold I bring to crown him again
> King forever ceasing never
> Over us all to reign.
>
> Frankincense to offer have I
> Incense owns a deity nigh
> Prayer and praising all men raising
> Worship him, God on high.
>
> Myrrh have I, its bitter perfume
> Breathes a life of gathering gloom
> Sorrowing, sighing, bleeding, dying,
> Sealed in a stone-cold tomb.
>
> O Star of Wonder, star of light
> Star with royal beauty bright
> Westward leading, still proceeding
> Guide us to thy glorious light.

DAY 17

A Son Given

> For unto us a child is born, unto us a son is given.
> —Isaiah 9:6 (ESV)
>
> He will be great and will be called the Son of the Most High …
> The child to be born will be called holy—the Son of God.
> —Luke 1:32, 35 (ESV)

I couldn't do it. Give my son away. Not for you, not for them, not for anyone. And I know you couldn't give yours away either.

It is for this very reason that possibly the most shocking aspect of Jesus's birth is this—He was a son given … unto us. And not just any son—though any son is unquestionably priceless. But this was the Son of the Most High … given … unto … *us*.

Mary is told by the angel that she will bear a son and call His name Jesus and that "He will be great and will be called the Son of the Most High" (Luke 1:32 ESV). When Mary, a virgin, wonders how this will come to pass, the angel continues, "The Holy Spirit will come upon you, and the power of the Most High will overshadow you; therefore the child to be born will be called holy—the Son of God" (Luke 1:35 ESV).

A child born—His humanity. But a Son given—His deity.

Such a deep mystery. The incarnation of the Son. He eternally existed, but this was the day He was begotten in human flesh. As is said many times over in Scripture, "You are my Son, today I have begotten you ... I will be to him a father, and he shall be to me a son" (Hebrews 1:5 ESV, Hebrews 5:5, Acts 13:13, Psalm 2:7, 89:26–27, 2 Samuel 7:14).

With wonder we ask along with the songwriter, "What child is this?"

And I think we need to move gently with this, as one might do when enveloping a newborn into one's arms—quietly, softly, reverently. It is in this spirit that I whisper *slowly* to you to consider ... how the Father ... sent His Son ... from the safeties of heaven ... to the perils of earth ... for us. How He sent His Son from the closest relationship in eternity to the inevitable separation of the cross ... for us. How, as a mother might transfer her sleeping babe into the cradled arms of another, He entrusted His precious, sweet, pure, holy Son into ours ... unto us.

The Son of the Most High. The Son whose position and place were beside His Father. Who had shared in the eternal glory that He had with the Father before the world existed (John 17:5). Who enjoyed such deep fellowship with His Father, He could say, "I and my Father are one" (John 10:30 NKJV, see also John 14:11, 17:21). The Son who was daily His Father's "delight, rejoicing before him always" (Proverbs 8:30 NKJV).

The Darling of Heaven ... given unto us.

Not pried from the Father's hand or wrestled from Him against His will or stolen from Him unawares but ... given. Freely gifted unto us.

And how have we responded to the giving of the Son? Have we cherished Him as His Father does? Is He "the one whom my soul loves," as the beloved bride of Solomon's Song would express? And I can faintly hear Him, there in the stillness of my heart, in the quiet of my spirit. That longing, gentle voice of the Son, asking of me what He asked of Peter so many years ago: "Do you *love* me? ... *Do* you love me? ... Do you love *Me*?" (John 21:15, 17 NKJV, my emphasis added). Would He have to ask me three times also? And were He to ask, would I be grieved as well? Like Peter, would I have to reply, "Lord, you know ... You know everything. You know that I love You."

So how have we done? Have we loved Him as our own?

When I entrust my children to my mother-in-law, she can hardly rest with the responsibility. I have complete peace and assurance that they are in the best of hands, because she treasures them as I treasure them, and she cares for them as if they were her own.

How have we done with the Son given to us? Have we valued Him as His Father does? Have we recognized the high honor and privilege in His having? History belies a poor legacy within humanity of carelessness and indeed, rejection of the Son given.

And each year at Christmas, do we sit casually in that armchair, glancing swiftly, thoughtlessly over the text: "For unto us a child is born, unto us a son is given"? Are we so used to the words that we don't really hear them anymore? Or do we get the memo but just not truly care? Or do we, perish the thought, think we actually deserve the gift of the Son? As though we are entitled to Him?

So maybe we need to press pause on this one. To stop in our tracks and really consider what it meant that "The Father sent his Son to be the Savior of the world" (1 John 4:14 NLT). Because we can't afford to overlook this generous gift. Our eternity depends on this—the giving of the Son. Not for a moment can we take Him for granted or pretend this was no big deal for God. There was so much at stake for us, and yet it was God who assumed all the risk when He didn't have to give us a thing, let alone His most prized possession—His Son.

Consider just how much God must love us if He was willing to invest His Son in us. How He sold all that He had to purchase us (Matthew 13:46). Take in how He plundered heaven for us, how He bankrupted Himself in giving His very life for us. "For you know the grace of our Lord Jesus Christ, that though he was rich, yet for your sake he became poor, so that you by his poverty might become rich" (2 Corinthians 8:9 ESV). What a baffling inversion.

John describes for us yet another confounding contradiction of how things are and how they ought to be when he writes, "In this is love, not that we have loved God but that he loved us and sent his Son to be the propitiation for our sins" (1 John 4:10 ESV). Not that we loved God?

We *should* have.

We had every reason to love God. We should have loved Him first and from day one, but we didn't. This is the first bewildering inversion. The second is this—that God loved us.

He *shouldn't* have.

He shouldn't have loved us at all. He had every last reason *not* to love us. But He did love us, and He loved us before we loved Him. That is the amazing contrast between how things are and how they ought to be. And He showed His unreasonable love for us in this way:

"Unto us a child is born, unto us a Son is given" (Isaiah 9:6 NKJV).

If we could only fully realize how much He loves us! And then meet His love with ours in return. The Son has told us, "The one who loves me will be loved by my Father, and I too will love them and show myself to them" (John 14:21 NIV). His love is most deeply experienced when it is received, and we love Him in return.

So, today may our hearts be hushed, our spirits grow quiet, and our souls be made soft as we honor the magnitude of what it meant that "God so loved the world that he gave his one and only Son" (John 3:16 NIV).

May we consider with thankfulness that "He ... did not spare his own Son but gave him up for us all" (Romans 8:32 NIV).

May we pause with humble gratitude for the eternal impact of how "God showed his love among us: He sent his one and only Son into the world that we might live through him" (1 John 4:9 NIV).

And just as you might open your arms to cradle a newborn when he is passed to you, just as you would receive that babe with all the care of a loving mother. Just as you might gently welcome him into the warmth of your arms, placing your hand softly on him. Just as you would ever so quietly enfold him and press him to your heart. Cherish the Son given, with open arms, contented heart, and grateful spirit.

> Silent night, holy night
> Son of God, love's pure light
> Radiant beams from Thy holy face
> With the dawn of redeeming grace
> Jesus, Lord, at Thy birth

DAY 18

The Accessible God

> And his name shall be called Wonderful Counselor.
> —Isaiah 9:6 (ESV)

There are those for whom Christmas is laced with pain.

It's a season that means joy and cheer to the masses but finds some individuals peering in through a window's glass from a cold, outside place. It means watching from the margins as others enjoy their families, receive their desired gifts, and surround themselves with all of life's finest comforts.

Christmas can be a lonely time of year for some.

On one hand, it might be a season that reminds some people of all the things they don't have and how they've come up short in life, a time that highlights the brokenness of their circumstances, the damage in family relationships, or the fading hope of unmet dreams.

On the other hand, some might "have it all" in a worldly sense or be considered blessed on many counts, but Christmastime reminds them of a loved one who should still be there to celebrate with them. And so, for these, Christmas brings with it a hollow ache inside.

When I was a child, our family lost our mother at Christmastime, and it took years to turn the tide of emptiness to the fullness we now enjoy.

So, the question is hard but honest: is Christmas only accessible to some? Does Christmas warm the hearts of most but mean heartache for a few? Will Christmas always be a highlight for many but heavily haunt some others?

My mind travels back to the time into which Jesus was born. Many descriptions surrounding His first advent make it clear to us that Jesus Messiah came to a hurting people, so in need of His wonderful counseling—His help, guidance, and wisdom. On so many levels they were a broken people in need of His healing and comfort. And God had taken note. He had seen their circumstances, He had heard the cries of their hearts, and He was moved with compassion for them.

Through the prophet Isaiah, God lovingly and beautifully expressed His heart's longing for His people:

"'Comfort, comfort my people,' says your God" (Isaiah 40:1 NLT).

So much desire in the repeating, "Comfort, comfort." And perhaps this is the reason George Frederick Handel begins his "Messiah" masterpiece with these very words. Of all the places in Scripture he could have begun, perhaps this was why he chose this passage—because the message of the Messiah comes from a place of comforting the broken and weary.

"Comfort, comfort my people, says your God. Speak tenderly to Jerusalem, and cry to her that her warfare is ended, that her iniquity is pardoned" (Isaiah 40:1–2 ESV). Then from this call to comfort, the Lord goes on to promise One who will provide this comfort, One who "will tend his flock like a shepherd; he will gather the lambs in his arms; he will carry them in his bosom, and gently lead those that are with young" (Isaiah 40:11 ESV).

Does it surprise you that the Mighty God comes to us so softly? That He comes to us as a shepherd? Or even as a babe? What comfort is gentler than a newborn? What tenderness is milder than a child? What kindness is sweeter than a baby? And the more one knows of God, the more one discovers the truth that He is "the Father of mercies and God of all comfort, who comforts us in all our affliction" (2 Corinthians 1:3–4 ESV). Yes, comfort is one of God's greatest ministries. He is the most excellent of counselors.

He is the One who speaks kindly to us with His gracious words, the One who has compassion on us and comforts our waste places—the hollow aching places of our souls, the One who comforts us in the valley of the shadow of death, and the One who finds a way to bring us comfort even when we refuse to be comforted. He is the One who comforts us with His promises, His Word, and His steadfast love, the One who comforts the afflicted, the downcast, and the storm-tossed. He comforts the mourner, as a mother would comfort her child. He is the One who comforts us with gladness and joy and with His peace, love, and hope.

And today, this One is drawing near to you with His assurance, "I, I AM he who comforts you" (Isaiah 51:12 ESV, my emphasis added).

You may not find comfort in Christmas—I AM he who comforts you.

You may not find comfort in family—I AM he who comforts you.

You may not find comfort in elusive dreams—I AM he who comforts you.

You may not find comfort in your loss—I AM he who comforts you.

You may not find comfort in your lack, your coming short, your never enough ... But today God is drawing near to tell you. "I AM he who comforts you."

I AM.

And how has He drawn near in comfort?

Through a child born. And a son given. The Wonderful

Counselor. The Wonderful *Comforter*. Yes, this One is that shepherd tending His flock. This Son given is the One carrying His lambs, those weakest among us, in His bosom. Those most in need of His tender, loving care. These are the ones He stoops down to lift up in His arms. They need not walk another step without Him, for He will carry them. And they will draw comfort from His heart beating against theirs.

Friend, are you one of those in need of such comfort?

He has come to you as the Wonderful Comforter. And He is here to tell you that Christmas is accessible to the brokenhearted.

It is accessible because there came a season to the God of all comfort when He was refused all comfort. This was no Christmas season. There were no gifts; there was no family, no warmth, no care. No, this season that came to our Savior was one of loneliness and heavy sorrow. The psalmist captures the anguish of this season: "Insults have broken my heart, and I am in despair. I waited for sympathy, but there was none; for comforters, but found no one" (Psalm 69:20 CSB). Alone, with no one to sympathize, He bore our sins and "carried our sorrows" (Isaiah 53:4 ESV).

And it is through His salvation that He is able to bring healing comfort to the heavy in heart. Perhaps this is the "consolation of Israel" that Simeon had been waiting for, as he looked on the Christ child and exclaimed, "My eyes have seen your salvation" (Luke 2:25, 30 ESV). It is God's salvation that brings the greatest comfort to the soul.

And I speak from experience. My mother's passing broke my heart. But two years later, when I was fifteen years of age, God saved me, and my heart began to heal. And now, along with all those who have experienced the comfort of God, we are "able to comfort those who are in any affliction, with the comfort with which we ourselves are comforted by God" (2 Corinthians 1:4 ESV).

It is in this manner that I ask those of you for whom Christmas is a season of joy, warmth, and plenty to look around you. Lift up your head, and scan your surroundings. Is there anyone you know who is in need of comfort? What could you do to share with them some of the comfort you enjoy at the hand of the God of all comfort?

Recently a friend of mine rallied a group of volunteers from our church to contribute items toward some beautiful gift baskets that she made up to bring to all the seniors of our church to cheer them during their lonely isolation this Christmas. She is one of the busiest people I know, but she's got her head up. She sees people. You and I similarly can be the means of God's comfort to someone *today*. Don't wait for Christmas. Make Christmas accessible to others today.

And finally, it brings joy to my heart to think of the promise Jesus left us before He returned to His Father. He told of a Comforter who would come to be with us always (John 14:16). In some translations, this One is called *Counselor*.

Wonderful Counselor.

No matter what season we are in, the Holy Spirit within us is able to bring His joy, peace, and comfort to our hearts.

May the Wonderful Counselor be your comfort this Christmas season.

> Oh tidings of comfort and joy
> Comfort and joy
> Oh tiding of comfort and joy

DAY 19

The Father God

> And his name shall be called ... Mighty God, Everlasting Father.
> —Isaiah 9:6 (ESV)

Do you want to know the real story behind Christmas? The "based on a true story" version of Christmas? Do you want the curtains of Bethlehem peeled back just a little and to peer into what was going on behind the scenes? All right, then we'll begin with a little clue.

This story begins with a Father's love.

That's what the real story is about: a Father's love for His Son and for His children. The true story is about the great lengths to which a Mighty God and an Everlasting Father would go to reach His wandering child. It's about a Father giving all that He had to find His lost child. It's about the Mighty God going beyond all boundaries of what is reasonable to rescue His child from peril. This, my friend, is the real story of Christmas. And the story begins many, many years before Bethlehem, long ago, at the dawn of time, before it all began, with the Mighty God ...

"In the beginning …" It reads so much like any story, doesn't it? But this is not just any story, this is *the* story! This is the story from which all other stories flow. Because "In the beginning, God" (Genesis 1:1 ESV). Full stop. "In the beginning" marks the moment when the Eternal met Time. When the Eternal *made* Time. God, the ever-existing One, creating time, space, and matter, in partnership with the Son. As John tells us, "In the beginning was the Word, and the Word was *with* God, and the Word *was* God. He was in the beginning with God. All things were made through him, and without him was not any thing made that was made" (John 1:1–3 ESV). John indicates for us that the Word—God's Son, Jesus Christ—was also eternal and preexisted His earthly birth. And thus, the story deepens already …

We tend to think of the Son as beginning in Bethlehem. History records His earthly beginning, so yes, it's true, as far as becoming human, Jesus had a beginning. But in His deity, Jesus existed long before Mary delivered Him into our world. He always was the Eternal Son of God. In John 17:5, Jesus speaks to His Father of "the glory that I had with you before the world existed" (ESV). Another time He declares to the Jews, "Truly, truly, I say to you, before Abraham was, I AM" (John 8:58 BLB, my emphasis added). In so doing, He claimed to be the Mighty God, preexisting Abraham, which is exactly who He is.

And so, the story of Christmas has a beginning far older than Bethlehem, far older than time! And as we await His coming during Advent, yes, we do reflect on His earthly beginning, His birth as a human babe, His flesh and blood entrance into our world. But we must never forget, He existed long before He arrived here on earth. Eternally, He was the Word. Eternally He is the Mighty God.

Yet as startling as His divinity is, what astounds me even more is His humanity! Oh yes, I can accept His deity without a doubt. I look around at creation and see the Creator. I peer into God's Word and see the Eternal Word. I view the life of Jesus and see the Christ.

I observe the miracles of Jesus and see the Mighty God. I have absolutely no issues with His divinity.

What leaves me amazed is His humanity.

It floors me to consider that "in him the whole fullness of deity dwells bodily" (Colossians 2:9 ESV). To harness the Mighty God into the body of a man is beyond understanding. To take the infinite greatness of all that God is and condense that into a baby—I can't fathom it. I am right there with Paul in wonder of this glorious truth, "Great indeed, we confess, is the mystery of godliness: He was manifested in the flesh" (1 Timothy 3:16 ESV). What an astonishing mystery! Can you explain it? Can you unpack that?

But it begs an even greater question—*Why*? Why would He come so low? Why become a man? Why bother with the likes of you and me? Why delight in humans? (Psalm 8:31). Why care anything about us? We are rebellious, godless, careless creatures. Why. On. Earth. Would. He. Come?

Because He's a father.

Because He's *the* Father.

Because He's the Everlasting Father.

That's why He came. Simply because He is the Everlasting Father. And what do fathers do? Fathers *love*, and fathers pursue. That's what fathers do. That's what fathers like God do. Regardless of the rebellion of their wandering children, fathers *love* them. Despite the carelessness of their children, fathers pursue them. Undeterred by the defiance of their children, fathers reach out to them. In spite of the ignorance of their children, fathers want to know them and be known by them.

Love needs no reasonable explanation. The Father's love for us is completely unreasonable, in fact. "God shows his love for us in that while we were still sinners, Christ died for us" (Romans 5:8 ESV). Who pours His love upon undeserving sinners? It's beyond rational explanation. And yet, there it is, the Father's love existing in all of its grace and truth, fully revealed to us in the person of His Son, Jesus Christ.

This is why "the Word became flesh and dwelt among us," so that we could *see, see, see* "his glory, glory as of the only Son from the Father, full of grace and truth" (John 1:14 ESV). So that we could witness all that the Everlasting Father is with our own two eyes, hear His words with our own two ears, touch His face with our own two hands.

As John affirms, "We proclaim to you the one who existed from the beginning, whom we have heard and seen. We saw him with our own eyes and touched him with our own hands. He is the Word of life" (1 John 1:1 NLT). A hands-on Father, you might say. The Father becoming tangible to us. The Eternal revealed in time. The Living Word, the Mighty God, the Everlasting Father, now made visible to us. Why?

Because He's a father, and He wants us to know Him. "And this is life eternal, that they know You, the only true God, and Jesus Christ whom You have sent" (John 17:3 NKJV). What a mystery indeed that God would reveal Himself to us. But the heart of the Father has always longed to be known by His children. The heart of the Father would go to any lengths to show Himself to His children, and so He poured Himself into that babe in a manger. He shone through the life of Christ (2 Corinthians 4:6). And shockingly, He completely lay bare and entirely exposed His love to us, in the death of His Son.

Oh, the aching, longing, loving, tender, merciful, gracious heart of the Everlasting Father, beating right before our eyes in the Person of Jesus Christ.

This is the real story of Christmas.

The Son making His Father known to us (John 1:18). The Son visibly representing the Father to us (John 12:45). The Son communicating the Father's character to us. The Son radiating God's own glory and expressing the very character of God to us (Hebrews 1:3). The Word, speaking God's grace and truth to us (John 1:14).

Philip once asked of Christ, "Lord, show us the Father," and Jesus replied, "Whoever has seen me has seen the Father" (John

14:8–9 ESV). Everything we need to know of the Everlasting Father is revealed to us in the Eternal Son. And above all things, He has revealed to us His love.

Have you looked into the face of that baby of Bethlehem and seen the Everlasting Father? Have you beheld there the countenance of the Mighty God? Have you followed the life of Christ and seen the Mighty God? Have you been to the cross and witnessed the love of the Everlasting Father?

Every story needs a conclusion. And every good story needs a happy ending—the kind where the lost child comes home, where the endangered child gets rescued, where the ignorant child at last desires the Father's company. God has given everything to express His love and desire for you—a Child born, a Son given. Can you express your love in return?

I know sometimes it's hard to find the words. Maybe we could start here ...

"Thanks be to God for his inexpressible gift!" (2 Corinthians 9:15 ESV).

> Christ by highest heaven adored
> Christ the Everlasting Lord
> Late in time behold Him come
> Offspring of the Virgin's womb
> Veiled in flesh, the Godhead see
> Hail, incarnate deity
> Pleased as man with man to dwell
> Jesus, our Emmanuel

DAY 20

Prince of Peace

> And the government shall be upon his shoulder, and his name shall be called ... Prince of Peace. Of the increase of his government and of peace there will be no end, on the throne of David and over his kingdom, to establish it and to uphold it with justice and righteousness from this time forth and forevermore.
> —Isaiah 9:6–7 (ESV)

> Glory to God in the highest and on earth peace among those with whom he is pleased!
> —Luke 2:14 (ESV)

Somehow, every soul knows that peace is the goal.

Constructs of utopia have always centered around peace and harmony, and people will go to great lengths and cost for inner peace and tranquility. With each passing year, the yearning for peace increases, but no matter what attempts are made, well-intentioned as they may be, the world always comes up dry on peace. One doesn't ever have to look far to see the glaring lack of peace in all realms of life—within nations, families, relationships, mental health, and ultimately, the soul. I think it's safe to say, the world is a troubled place and in deep need of the Prince of Peace.

You may have heard the saying: "Peace is not found in the absence of problems; it is found in the presence of God." And that's good, but my question is, why? Why is peace found in the presence of God rather than in the absence of problems? How is it that God brings peace to us in spite of our circumstances? And how will He bring lasting peace to our world? If the only definition of peace still allows for the presence of problems—the result of sin's curse—then is that a complete peace? Is there not a peace yet to be had for our world where there is, yes, the presence of God but also an absence of problems?

Because if there isn't, then I most certainly echo the dismay of that one who "heard the bells on Christmas day,"

> And in despair I bowed my head
> There is no peace on earth I said
> For hate is strong and mocks the song
> Of peace on earth, good will to men.

Now, our current lack of world peace and peace in the world cannot be the fault of the Prince or His Peace. Both are perfect. So, where is the holdup? The message of the angels clearly promised peace on earth (Luke 2:14). But you'll find there is more than one facet to the Prince's peace. There's His reconciling peace, His righteous peace, and His ruling peace. In His first coming, Jesus did bring reconciling peace to this earth in that He made a way for us to have peace with God by the blood of His cross.

So, in this sense, there are always those "on earth," at all times, who do know peace with God. And these saved ones are then called to be administrators of His righteous peace here and now. (There is a fascinating correlation all through Scripture between righteousness and peace.) But I don't think anyone can claim we've arrived at global peace. So, Christ's farthest-reaching peace, His ruling peace, must still be coming.

It is in Christ's second coming where lasting peace will come at last to the earth by way of the Prince of Peace and His righteous government. "The government shall be upon his shoulder ... Of the increase of his government and of peace there will be no end" (Isaiah 9:6 ESV). It will be a beautiful reign like no other: "In his days may the righteous flourish, and peace abound ... May he have dominion ... to the ends of the earth" (Psalm 72:7–8 ESV).

His title as Prince is also significant. Not only is He the principal peacemaker, but He is also its highest-ranking authority. And princes are those who have dominion and rule. He has already earned the right to rule through His sacrifice but is still "waiting ... until his enemies should be made a footstool for his feet" (Hebrews 10:12–13 ESV, see also Hebrews 1:13, Psalm 110:1, Matthew 22:44, Acts 2:34–36). Only once "God has put all things in subjection under his feet" (1 Corinthians 15:28 ESV), under the rule of the Prince of Peace will there ever be "world peace."

You see, perfect peace operates in the realm of righteous rule, which is why on a micro-, current-day level, we are told to pray for kings and those in authority, so that we may lead peaceful lives (1 Timothy 2:1–2). But unlike flawed worldly rulers, who can be unjust and might inflict terror, the Prince of Peace is perfect, and His rule will be characterized by peace and perfect justice—everything your soul longs for, the world you know is supposed to be, but you can't see right now because of the chaos and disorder sin has brought. Yes, His rule will bring about everything the world longs for right now, but sadly, the world refuses to be ruled by Christ. It wants the gift of peace but not the Prince of Peace. Herein lays our greatest problem.

He is coming to rule though. And how will He do it? Not easily. The Prince does not come by His Peace easily. Peace is a battle hard fought, and it only follows war, which is why in Scripture, "peace" is often accompanied by military language, such as *guard*, *rule*, *dominion, armor, kingdom, crush, alienated, hostile, reconciled, kings, high places, disciplined, trained, strive, equip, conquer, put under foot, pursue.* Not exactly a peaceful night's sleep, is it?

The cross is where the Prince fought and won His hardest battle. Through this victory, He was able to make our peace with God in salvation, reconciling two hostile parties by conquering sin—the root of all hostility. And along with that, He has opened the way to bring lasting peace everywhere—"to reconcile to himself all things, whether on earth or in heaven, making peace by the blood of his cross" (Colossians 1:20 ESV).

The day will come when His righteous peace will encompass everything, and then in *all* the earth and heavens, there will be peace. There will be no trace of sin or its problematic consequences ever again. An absence of problems and also the presence of God—perfect, permanent peace.

I believe this truth is what restores hope to our caroling friend from earlier:

> Then pealed the bells more loud and deep,
> God is not dead, nor doth He sleep
> The wrong shall fail, the right prevail
> With peace on earth, goodwill to man.

So, what about us, then, in the here and now? Is the Prince of Peace only interested in His coming reign? Not at all. The peace He won for His coming kingdom when He died on the cross starts with us *today*. The legal right and access to His peace is ours now. "Since we have been justified by faith, we have peace with God through our Lord Jesus Christ" (Romans 5:1 ESV). His peace is not yet on *all* the earth or in *all* the world, but it is found in the domain of the hearts of those "with whom he is pleased"—those who accept the Christ who is born Savior (Luke 2:14 ESV). All the groundwork for peace has already been laid at the cross, and because we know the God of peace, we can also know the peace of God in our lives (Philippians 4:7–9).

Even when the world around us is in turmoil and circumstances rock our boat, we can be kept in His perfect peace (Isaiah 26:3). He says, "In me you may have peace" (John 16:33 ESV). "Peace I leave with you; my peace I give to you. Not as the world gives ... Let not your hearts be troubled, neither let them be afraid" (John 14:27 ESV). *He* is our peace (Ephesians 2:14). He is the One who brings order into the chaos of life, because wherever the Prince of Peace reigns, there is peace.

Yes, peace comes where Christ rules, which is why Paul implores, "Let the peace of Christ rule in your hearts" (Colossians 3:15 ESV). So, I would challenge myself—does Christ rule in my heart? Does He have dominion in my life today? I don't have to wait until a future day to honor Him as Prince of Peace.

If there is any area of my life in which I am not experiencing His peace, could it be that I am not submitting it to His rule? If I won't be ruled by the Prince of Peace, then I won't know the peace of the Prince.

And I know it's difficult to relinquish the throne of your life. It's hard to submit your anxious thoughts, your fears, your desires, and your own will to His rule. No one likes to be ruled. Nobody wants to be governed. But the guarantee of His peace is worth it.

And on this peaceful note, we conclude. While the work to achieve peace is warlike, the results of peace are that of a garden. The imagery in Scripture is obvious in this way. Scripture speaks almost poetically of how "the fruit of the Spirit is ... peace" (Galatians 5:22 ESV); how discipline "yields the peaceful fruit of righteousness" (Hebrews 12:11 ESV); how "the wisdom from above is first pure, then peaceable ... full of ... good fruits" (James 3:17 ESV); and how "a harvest of righteousness is sown in peace by those who make peace" (James 3:18 ESV). It might be a stretch, but I don't think it is—could such fruitful language be an allusion to His coming rule of peace? To the new heavens and the new earth, flourishing with the abundant fruit of His righteousness, the fruit of the Spirit—love, joy, and *peace*—under the rule of the Prince of Peace?

We can know a little of this heaven today on earth. Enthrone the Prince of Peace today in your heart and reap a harvest of His wonderful, lasting peace that is only ever found in Christ.

"Now may the Lord of peace himself give you peace at all times in every way" (2 Thessalonians 3:16 ESV).

> He rules the world with truth and grace
> And makes the nations prove
> The glories of His righteousness
> And wonders of His love

DAY 21

The Star and the Scepter

> *A Star shall come out of Jacob; a Scepter shall rise out of Israel.*
> —Numbers 24:17 (NKJV)

Our family had been buzzing with excitement over a star that was set to appear its brightest on December 21 of 2020—the winter solstice—and then was supposed to shine right through Christmas week. What could have been a more perfect collision of events? A Christmas star at Christmastime. And to round off 2020, no less. It did make me wonder at the timing of it all. The year 2020 had been such a hard one for our world; it was bound to be so heartening to see this star brighten our nights during the Christmas season. Maybe this year, we will be spoiled again! But I am quite certain it will be another half century before such an occurrence happens again.

Regardless, my prayer for this year is that another Star will brighten our hearts this season. The Star of Jacob. O, the hope in His rising! May He ascend to the highest pinnacle in our souls!

This Star coming out of Jacob is of course the Lord Jesus Christ, as prophesied thousands of years before He was born: "A Star will come out of Jacob; a Scepter will rise out of Israel" (Numbers 24:17 NKJV). At the time of His birth, it was to the magi that His star first appeared in the sky, leading them to *the* Star of Jacob. The magi witnessed His star's rising and responded with faith to the heavens' declaration of the glory of God and the sky's proclamation of God's handiwork (Psalm 19:1). What glory they were about to encounter shining in the face of Jesus Christ. What handiwork they were soon to witness in this child, the newborn King.

You know, there's a story behind today's text, this prophecy from Numbers 24. And it would be funny if it weren't so pathetic. An enemy of Israel had hired a wicked prophet named Balaam to curse Israel from a high mountain overlooking the vast desert camp of the Israelites. Ironically, every time Balaam opened his mouth to curse Israel, God took control of his mouth, and he could only speak beautiful words of blessing over Israel, much to the consternation of both Balaam and his employer. This prophecy is part of a series of amazing promises God gave to Israel as spoken through Balaam.

Despite its deplorable messenger, this prophecy and the circumstances under which it was given is cause for great hope. No matter how hard the enemy tries to thwart God's plan, the Star *will* come and the Scepter *will* rise! Indeed, the Star has come and the Scepter has risen, in full keeping with God's promise.

This promise was not new to Israel. Hundreds of years prior to Balaam's prophecy, their forefather and namesake, Israel, also known as Jacob, prophesied these words: "The scepter will not depart from Judah, nor the ruler's staff from his descendants, until the coming of the one to whom it belongs, the one whom all nations will honor" (Genesis 49:10 NLT).

This Scepter, just as the Star, speaks of Christ, the One to whom all power and authority and ultimate rule will be given, as King of kings and Lord of lords.

I am reminded of the implications of a rising scepter from the story of Esther. We learn that the power of the king to judge between life and death lies in the scepter. Esther's life, and her fear of going in before the king, hinged on his scepter rising or falling. It might not rise to welcome her, which would mean her immediate death. One can imagine Esther's great relief when she sees the king's scepter rise to greet her, welcoming her in before him and ensuring the safety of her life. It is the risen scepter that grants her access before his throne.

Imagine God raising His scepter to us?

I am fully aware that His Scepter rising indicates the ascension of Christ to the eternal throne. But the imagery is not lost on me as I read of Esther and think of my own standing before His awesome presence. I cannot help but think of His scepter rising to me in the mercy and grace of His salvation.

I am completely humbled by this. That Scepter that should have called for my judgment and condemnation became the very source of my salvation and acceptance before the King. Yes, God would never raise His scepter to us on a whim, overlooking His justice that must be satisfied. His righteous demands had to be met for us to gain entrance before Him. And these demands are met by the Scepter, Jesus Christ, so that He might raise His scepter to us.

But the path by which He rose as the Scepter was also not by whim. It was no small thing for Christ to rise to the throne of His father David. He had to overcome our sin, death, and the grave.

And so, the Scepter rises on a cross. The One who would rule with power and authority first must rise upon a cross, "that through death he might destroy the one who has the power of death, that is the devil, and deliver all those who through fear of death were subject to lifelong slavery" (Hebrews 2:14–15 ESV). In rising upon the cross, He disarmed any would-be authorities, making "a public spectacle of them, triumphing over them by the cross" (Colossians 2:15 NKJV). Oh yes, there will only be one Scepter rising!

Then the Scepter rises from the tomb. He rises from the dead, as the victorious conqueror over sin, death, and the grave. "The last enemy to be destroyed is death" (1 Corinthians 15:26 ESV). And He does defeat death in His rising from "death, because it was not possible for him to be held by it" (Acts 2:24 ESV). Suffice to say, "death no longer has dominion over him" (Romans 6:9 ESV). Remember, He is the one who holds all the power and authority now. And His resurrection provides profound hope for those who trust in Him, because if He has risen, then we too will rise with Him (Romans 8:11; 1 Corinthians 6:14, 15:12–17; 2 Corinthians 4:14; Ephesians 2:5–6).

And at last, the Scepter rises to the throne. Soon He will rise to the eternal throne of His father David. "The Lord God will give him the throne of his father David, and he will reign ... forever" (Luke 1:32–33 ESV). And God will also give Him the scepter: "But of the Son he says, 'Your throne, O God, is forever and ever, the scepter of uprightness is the scepter of your kingdom'" (Hebrews 1:8 ESV, see also Psalm 45:6). Christ has earned the right to take the eternal throne and hold the scepter. And His Father delights to give Him the kingdom: "The Lord sends forth from Zion your mighty scepter. Rule in the midst of your enemies!" (Psalm 110:2 ESV). "Judah is my scepter" (Psalm 60:7 and 108:8 ESV).

And so ... a Scepter rises.

He has proven worthy and able to rule and to hold the power. And He is also now able to justly and graciously raise the scepter to us to draw near unafraid.

The Star *will* rise; the Scepter *will* rise. And soon the Morning Star—Jesus Christ—will rise when He comes for those who love Him (2 Peter 1:19, Revelation 22:16). And it is the hope of the church that soon we will rise to meet Him, and from then on, we will always be with Him (1 Thessalonians 4:16–17). A bright future for sure.

So, how do you want to finish this year? God has given us every reason to step into the New Year with worship and praise.

We don't need to finish in defeat and despair, pining away in the darkness. I couldn't help but be touched during Christmas 2020 by that beautiful star shining in our winter skies. Not seen since 1226—almost eight hundred years! And there it shone in a year when our world had had its very heart broken and was in great need of brightening.

But something greater shines—the Star of Jacob! Will you be captured by His radiance? Will you bow to His risen scepter? Will you look with expectation for the rising of the Morning Star? Let's make this Christmas one that is full of love, joy, peace, and praise—rejoicing with "a thrill of hope"!

> O holy night, the stars are brightly shining
> It is the night of our dear Savior's birth
> Long lay the world in sin and error pining
> Till he appeared and the soul felt its worth
> A thrill of hope the weary world rejoices
> For yonder breaks a new and glorious morn
> Fall on your knees, O hear the angel voices!
> O night divine! O holy night when Christ was born

DAY 22

The Root-Shoot

> There shall come forth a shoot from the stump of Jesse, and a branch from his roots shall bear fruit. And the Spirit of the Lord shall rest upon him ... In that day the root of Jesse, who shall stand as a signal for the peoples—of him shall the nations inquire, and his resting place shall be glorious.
> —Isaiah 11:1–2, 10 (ESV)

> I am the Root and Offspring of David.
> —Revelation 22:16 (NKJV)

> For nothing will be impossible with God.
> —Luke 1:27 (ESV)

The Christmas story is really a story that magnifies all that is possible with God.

It's a story that presents a myriad of impossibilities that require God's miraculous intervention to bring into being. It reaches even further back than ancient Abraham and the promise that his offspring would be heirs of the world, that in him all nations would be blessed (Romans 4:13; Genesis 18:18, 22:18; Galatians 3:8, 16). Humanly speaking, this was an impossibility. Abraham and his barren, aging wife had no son and heir of their own, let alone one for the whole world!

Impossible with man, yes, but not impossible with God. God glories with stepping into the impossible and then accomplishing what only He can do. He delights with breathing into deadness and raising to life His promises. And so, by faith, Abraham believed God, "who gives life to the dead and calls into existence the things that do not exist. In hope he believed against hope" (Romans 4:17 ESV). Against all the odds, Abraham believed the impossible. Correction—he believed the *God* of the impossible.

Paul tells us that Abraham "gave glory to God, fully convinced that God was able to do what he had promised" (Romans 4:20–21 ESV). So, from the fruitless womb of Sarah comes forth a son, a living testament to this truth that "nothing will be impossible with God" (Luke 1:27 ESV). And if we were to start in Matthew chapter 1 and read through the genealogy of Jesus, we would find that the family tree begins with Abraham and culminates with Christ—the Promised One, the Child who would fulfill God's humanly impossible promise to Abraham.

Which brings us to Jesus and the impossible circumstances of His own birth. Isaiah primed us for the miraculous when he foretold, "The Lord himself will give you a sign. Behold, a virgin shall conceive and bear a son, and shall call his name Immanuel" (Isaiah 7:14 ESV). And so, we are introduced to Mary, a virgin, who "was found to be with child from the Holy Spirit" (Matthew 1:18 ESV).

Luke expands on the details and tells us that the "angel Gabriel was sent from God ... to a virgin ... And the virgin's name was Mary" (Luke 1:26–27 ESV). Gabriel explains to her, "You will conceive in your womb and bear a son, and you shall call his name

Jesus ... The Holy Spirit will come upon you, and the power of the Most High will overshadow you; therefore, the child to be born will be called holy—the Son of God" (Luke 1:26 and 35 ESV).

And as an assurance of these things, Gabriel informs her of yet another impossible pregnancy—that of her barren cousin Elizabeth. "Behold, your relative Elizabeth in her old age has also conceived a son ... who was called barren. For nothing will be impossible with God" (Luke 1:36–37 ESV). It is just so like God to transform what is barren into that which is fruitful, to resurrect life from death.

It is to this hopeful end that God raises a shoot from the stump of Jesse, as per our Scripture reading from today. What life can come from a stump? Cut down almost to the root, it appears to be all but dead—nothing to grow upward, no branches to provide shelter or provision. New growth is a near impossibility.

But the marvel is this—a shoot does spring forth from the stump. Jesus Christ says of Himself, "I am the Root and Offspring of David" (Revelation 22:16 NKJV). Christ is the One who fulfills God's promises to David as his offspring: "There shall come forth a shoot from the stump of Jesse, and a branch from his roots shall bear fruit" (Isaiah 11:1 ESV). Imagine so much life coming from something nearly dead? Who was Jesse anyway? Was there anything about him of significance, if not for God raising King David from his house? And who was David? Was he not the forgotten youngest son of Jesse? Overlooked and demeaned by his older brothers? Dumped in the fields to do the work of a lowly shepherd? A stump.

And yet it is the way of our God to take a stump—overlooked, insignificant, forgotten, small—and from that dead end to bring forth life in abundance.

What realm of your life is the impossible, friend? Where does your stump lie? What root have you given up on? May the Lord be gracious to you and revive His purpose in you by the power of His hand alone. May He do a work in your life and in mine that is only of His miraculous making. May He do the impossible for His honor and glory!

Yes, from that dead-end stump of Jesse, the Messiah came. Long after David's throne had been abandoned and all would-be kings descending from David's line had been forced to abdicate. It seemed impossible to recover the throne. Jesse's house had been cut down to the very root, David's royal heritage all but lost. Until, after centuries of dormancy, a King springs forth, born "in the city of David" (Luke 2:11 ESV). From the fruit of Mary's womb comes the tender shoot. "And the Lord God will give him the throne of his father David, and he will reign over the house of Jacob, and of his kingdom there will be no end" (Luke 1:32–33 ESV).

His kingdom is coming. The promise still stands to Israel and Judah: "Behold, the days are coming, declares the Lord, when I will raise up for David a righteous Branch, and he shall reign as king and deal wisely, and shall execute justice and righteousness in the land" (Jeremiah 23:5 ESV, see also Jeremiah 33:15, Zechariah 3:8). "Thus says the Lord of hosts, 'Behold, the man whose name is the Branch ... shall bear royal honor, and shall sit and rule on his throne" (Zechariah 6:12–13 ESV). "In that day the branch of the Lord shall be beautiful and glorious" (Isaiah 4:2 ESV).

This One will also bring hope to the Gentiles, yet another supposed impossibility in the minds of the Jews. Paul quotes Isaiah when he says, "The root of Jesse will come, even he who arises to rule the Gentiles; in him will the Gentiles hope" (Romans 15:12 ESV, see also Isaiah 11:10), thus, fulfilling God's promise to Abraham that in him all the world would be blessed, bringing us full circle. So much life and blessing has been brought to Jew and Gentile because of this Root of David (Revelation 5:5). The impossible made possible.

"For nothing will be impossible with God" (Luke 1:27 ESV).

God works in the realm of the impossible to make His glory known and to amplify the greatness of His works. He employs the weak, the feeble, the inadequate, and the nearly dead, because then, as we "hope against all hope," God brings to life something of His making alone. And while we watch with wonder and amazement, we simply say, along with Mary, "Behold, I am the Lord's servant; let it be to me according to your word" (Luke 1:38 ESV).

> O come, Thou Rod of Jesse, free
> Thine own from Satan's tyranny ...
> O come, Thou key of David, come
> And open wide our heavenly home ...
> Rejoice! Rejoice! Emmanuel
> Shall come to thee, O Israel.

DAY 23

The Lion Lamb

> Behold, the Lion of the tribe of Judah, the
> Root of David, has conquered.
> —Revelation 5:5 (ESV)

> Behold, you will ... bear a son, and you shall call
> his name Jesus. He will be great ... And the Lord
> will give him the throne of his father David.
> —Luke 2:31–32 (ESV)

"Mom?" a little voice called out to me from the back of the car.

Handel's "Messiah" had been filling the vehicle with its angelic chords, weaving its way through the wonders and woe of the story of the Christ, stretching from eternity past to the far reaches of His future reign. It is always a favorite of mine to play at Christmastime. We had come to the final movement of Handel's masterpiece, and in all of its thundering glory, the words of Scripture strained forth above the orchestra, *"Worthy is the Lamb that was slain ..."*

Again, a little voice called out from the back of the car, "Mom? Can you turn it up, please? ... It sounds like heaven!"

Ah, but how did she know? Had I mentioned it before? Had she heard these words previously in some Sunday morning sermon? How did this little child know the sound of heaven is that of praise resounding to the Lamb?

I have always been struck to the core by that scene in Revelation 5 where the call goes out to all of earth and sky—"Who is worthy to open the scroll and break its seals?" And on the inside, I cry along with John as he weeps. And sometimes I cry on the outside too, at the heartbreaking hopelessness of no one in heaven or on earth or under the earth "found worthy to open the scroll or to look into it" (Revelation 5:2–4 ESV).

This is a story of all hope lost and in great need of restoring. It is a scene that forces us to consider the great "What If?" What if no one is found worthy? What if no one is able to right the wrongs of the world and usher in the kingdom? The hopelessness in John's weeping reflects all of the despair of a world that won't be righted—one in which the kingdom may not come, sin is left unpunished, the wicked prevail, suffering is unending, and sorrows are unhealed. Does this unravel the whole story of Christmas, which hinges completely on the hope of Christ's coming kingdom?

Because let's face it. Sometimes it is hard to find Him. Sometimes a great search must be made. Sometimes the call must go out, "Is there anyone who is able?" Is there anyone? Are you there, Lord? Do you see what is happening? All seems lost! And my hope is gone! I have nothing left but my tears.

But just because He can't be seen doesn't mean He isn't there. Just because He seems hard to find doesn't mean He is absent. Just because my sight is dim doesn't mean He isn't present. As John is about to discover ...

Just when all hope is lost, it happens. At that moment of greatest despair, hope ignites. An elder encourages John, "Weep no more; behold, the Lion of the tribe of Judah, the Root of David, has conquered, so that he can open the scroll" (Revelation 5:5 ESV). Yes, hope arises! Like a phoenix rising from the ashes, hope takes flight! Someone has been found worthy! Someone is able to open the scroll. He's been there all along! Right there in our presence, by the throne, beside the creatures, among the elders. He's been with us. A *Lion*! No less. The *Lion* from the tribe of Judah. From Judah, the one who means praise. From the tribe of the kings. He has been found worthy! And yes, we will praise Him!

We know this Lion. We've tracked this Lion from His first introduction in Scripture, from the first mention of any lion in Scripture: "Judah is a lion's cub: from the prey, my son, you have gone up … who dares rouse him? The scepter shall not depart from Judah, nor a ruler's staff from between his feet" (Genesis 49:9–10 ESV). Yes! This is Him! The hope of all nations! Of course, this would be the One to conquer. The fearsome Lion. Who dares rouse him? Yes, who dares cross the powerful, mighty Lion of the tribe of Judah? This is our conqueror! This is our King!

But then strangely, John says, there "between the throne and the four living creatures and among the elders I saw a Lamb" (Revelation 5:6 ESV). A Lamb? But this is not possible. We were told the One who is worthy is the Lion. The conqueror is the Lion. How is it that we now see a Lamb? And furthermore, "A Lamb standing, as though it had been slain" (Revelation 5:6 ESV)? A slain Lamb? What could be weaker? What could be more defeated? A slain yet risen Lamb? How is *this* our Lion?

Ah, but in truth, why are we so surprised? Did we not witness this very paradox in His first coming, at His birth? We awaited the promise of the Lion of Judah, but what did we receive? A baby wrapped in the swaddling cloths of a sacrificial Passover lamb. At Christ's first advent, the Lion of Judah came to us in the body of a newborn babe. What a wonder.

Then, years later, John introduced Him to us as "the Lamb of God" who would take "away the sin of the world!" (John 1:29 ESV). Raised on a cross, Christ hung beneath this inscription, "The King of the Jews" (John 19:19 ESV). The King—the Lion of Judah—the sacrificial Lamb of God.

And as we weave our way through Scripture and trace the path of the Lion, we begin to discover a mystery—the Lion of Judah always presents as the Lamb of God. And the Lamb of God always displays the courage and dignity of the Lion of Judah.

On the one hand, we see Jesus "led as a lamb to the slaughter" (Isaiah 53:7 NKJV), willingly stepping into death. On the other hand—on the other side of Calvary—we witness His foes hiding themselves, as though from a lion but in truth, from the wrath of the Lamb (Revelation 6:16). The Lamb, who opens the seals of judgment, wars with His enemies and conquers every adversary as the Lord of lords and King of kings (Revelation 17:14). The King who is the Lamb. The Lion Lamb. What a mystery.

And I do understand the incongruity of it all. Under the effects of the curse, nature has set lion against lamb, in direct opposition with each other, constantly at odds with one another as predator and prey. But in God's original design, there is no such conflict. This conflict came by way of the curse of sin.

Currently, creation reflects the nature of fallen man, not the nature of the Lion Lamb. But one day, even creation will be freed from the effects of the curse and will once again reflect the nature of the Lion Lamb. And in that day, lion shall lie down with lamb in perfect harmony (Isaiah 11:6, 65:25). In complete consistency with the Lion Lamb.

Which brings us back to that heavenly scene. John is fortified with the angel's encouraging discovery that One has been found worthy to open the scroll and loose the seal. Yes, the Lion from the tribe of Judah, He has prevailed! He has conquered! As the slain yet resurrected Lamb of God. And all hope is restored!

Maybe, like John, we too need to look up from our despair and discover the hope we have in the Lamb. Maybe we too need to see *between*, as John did, and recall the arrival of the Lion to Bethlehem's manger as a precious Lamb. Do we love Him? And to turn once again to Calvary and see by faith—within the bowed head of the crucified Lamb of God—the Lion of the tribe of Judah. Can we see Him? And to rejoice in His resurrection power, conquering sin and death and hell. Do we know it? And to freshly glimpse the victorious Lion Lamb, who is found worthy and able. Do we praise Him? And to rest in the deep hope that He delivers. Do we embrace it? And as we savor the moment ...

We hear all of heaven break into a new song, "Worthy is the lamb who was slain, to receive power and wealth and wisdom and might and honor and glory and blessing!" (Revelation 5:12 ESV). We see all of heaven fall down and worship the Lamb who sits upon the throne!

And that little voice—the voice of one of His very own precious little lambs—calls out from the back of my car, "Turn it up, Mom! ... It sounds like heaven!"

> And heaven and nature sing
> And heaven and nature sing
> And heaven, and heaven and nature sing!

DAY 24

Joy to the World

> Behold, I bring you *good news* of *great joy* that will be for *all* the people. For unto you is born this day in the city of David a Savior, who is Christ the Lord.
> —Luke 2:10–11 (ESV, my emphasis added)

It's been quite the journey, this.

Not one I could have planned or mapped out on my own. It began as a thought, the words rolling through my mind in those weeks prior to writing—"Awaiting His Coming." My soul was in need of something deep that Advent and still is. The year I initially wrote these reflections, because of pandemic restrictions, there wasn't to be the usual festive parties or even the demanding yet enjoyable church Christmas program. The world around was filled with doom and gloom, and my heart was longing for something it needed. Christ.

What began as a thought became a gentle nudging. I can only describe it as being a wind at my back, softly but assuredly pressing me forward. *What if you stepped deeply into the waiting?* Oh, there are a thousand books on Advent I could have been reading this season. I have plenty, lined up neatly on the bookshelf. Each one compelling. *But what if this year you just opened one book?* The *book?*

And then came the unexpected. "What if you were to share this journey with others?" Gasp. But the pressure of having material. The constant bombardment of daily content. The lack of a detailed plan. The what-ifs, and I-can't, and are-you-sure? But the vision just grew, and I knew this … was … happening. Into the unknown. Just the Holy Spirit, the Word, and me … and you. Thank you so much for joining me!

And what a journey it has been, let me tell you! The things He has shown me! I've laughed. I've cried. I've headed down some paths, only to be pushed toward something entirely the opposite—more beautiful and amazing than I could have ever come up with on my own. I've been daily blown away by this great and wonderful God and His great and wonderful plan!

I have often wondered in the past what on earth Moses did for those forty days up in the mountain with God. I just might have a small idea now. If eternity is anything like the presence of God we can experience here below, then, bring it on!

I saw a pattern of His own making beginning to emerge over the weeks. I'm usually one to studiously plan things well in advance, to fine-tune the course outline before heading out. But because of the in-the-moment nature of this adventure, I had to trust His plan. Beautifully, we began with the human and moved to the divine. In the beginning, my reflections drew upon the human story of Christmas. But gradually I was brought closer to Christ's deity. So like God to draw us *up*.

We have covered some interesting territory these past weeks, ranging from somber to touching to uplifting to challenging, and it has left me wondering all along where we would end. Would we be left on a serious note right before Christmas Day or high upon a mountain peak? It gradually became clearer—we must end with *joy!*

Yes, of course! *Joy* to the world! The Lord *has* come! What better note to end on than the experience of *joy* at His coming! The story of the Nativity is punctuated with *joy*. One can hardly turn the page without running into *joy*. *Joy* almost becomes another character in the story! It is seen everywhere! And a theme begins to take shape. Anyone who encounters the Christ, anyone who meets the Lord, finds *joy*!

Jesus had not even been born yet. He was mere conception when Mary traveled to visit her cousin Elizabeth, who was also expecting a child. When Mary greeted her, Elizabeth "was filled with the Holy Spirit, and she exclaimed with a loud cry, 'Blessed are you among women, and blessed is the fruit of your womb! And why is this granted to me that the mother of my Lord should come to me? For behold, when the sound of your greeting came to my ears, the baby in my womb leaped for joy'" (Luke 1:41–44 ESV).

Mary hadn't even *told* Elizabeth she was expecting the Messiah. And Mary would certainly not be showing yet. How did Elizabeth know? The Holy Spirit revealed it to her. But something else wonderful happened as well—the baby Elizabeth was carrying in her womb *leaped for joy*! Can you imagine it? An unborn child is one of the first to recognize the unborn Messiah! Unbelievable. What a miracle! And how is it that an unborn child could experience *joy*? Let that sit for a while ... And so, it is that Jesus, not yet born, is already spreading *joy* in His coming.

Without a doubt, Elizabeth's Spirit-filled greeting would have caused Mary's own spirit to lift. Someone believed and understood the truth surrounding her pregnancy, but more than that, Elizabeth embraced the nature of who the child was—the Lord! The Messiah! And so Mary's heart exults in praise and worship: "My soul magnifies the Lord, and my spirit rejoices in God my Savior" (Luke 1:46–47 ESV). She then goes on to praise the Lord for His mighty works, His holy name, His enduring mercy, His arm of strength, His provision, and the fulfillment of His promises to Abraham's offspring (Luke 1:48–55). So much *joy* at Christ's coming!

Joy then takes us out into the cold, dark hills surrounding Bethlehem, to the shepherds, "keeping watch over their flock by night" (Luke 2:8 ESV). The angel appears to them and says, "Fear not, for behold, I bring you good news of *great joy* that will be for all the people. For unto you is born this day in the city of David a Savior, who is Christ the Lord ... Glory to God in the highest, and on earth peace" (Luke 2:8–11, 14 ESV).

Good news of great *joy*! I don't know of any news that could bring more joy than that of Christ's coming! The hope of the Messiah, the salvation that He would bring, was cause for great joy! And this joy has continued to reach the hearts and souls of men and women, boys and girls, right into this day and age. There is no greater joy than to receive the good news, His gospel! How blessed are we?

These humble shepherds could hardly contain themselves. In short, they didn't. "And when they saw it, they made known the saying that had been told them, concerning the child. And all who heard it wondered at what the shepherds told them ... And the shepherds returned, glorifying and praising God for all they had heard and seen, as it had been told them" (Luke 2:17–20 ESV).

Such is the *joy* of Christ's coming that it bursts the heart! This is good news of goodwill that we cannot keep to ourselves! And when Simeon and Anna meet Jesus in the temple, they too are left praising and thanking God and speaking of Him to all who awaited the Messiah! *Joy*, by its very nature, overflows to all around.

Many months later, the wise men arrive from their long journey to meet the King. Their search had met with some obstacles and could have sent them home disappointed—except "the star that they had seen when it rose went before them until it came to rest over the place where the child was. When they saw the star, they rejoiced exceedingly with great joy" (Matthew 2:9–10 ESV). They rejoiced because their search was over, and at last, they would meet the child!

Matthew can't record the moment with any more *joy* than he has packed into that little verse: "*rejoiced exceedingly* with *great joy*" (Matthew 2:10 ESV, my emphasis added). If we could employ exclamation marks, this is where I would put them! Step into their moment, friend. Imagine journeying endlessly by camel, traveling through a grueling desert, searching for months and months and some more long, weary months and then finally arriving at the Christ. Not a far cry from our own journey through the long, weary months of this past year. Can you imagine the *joy*? So. Much. *Rejoicing*!

My mind travels back to the time when I first met the King. My King. I was just a girl of fifteen. Troubled, unhappy, angry, confused. All the makings of a grieving teenage girl. That's how I came to the King. Crying on the inside. But everything changed the moment we met! There couldn't have been a greater transformation to joy than the one that occurred in my heart!

My first thought upon trusting Christ was this: "There is *joy* in the presence of the angels of God over one sinner who repents" (Luke 15:10 NIV, my emphasis added). I thought of my mother in the presence of the angels and wondered if she too was rejoicing. I remember also the night of my baptism, my cheeks sore with smiling. There amid my own joy, I could hear the soaring of my dad's voice above all the others, "Oh happy day!"

Christ the King has been my *joy* ever since!

Do you know the *joy* of meeting the Christ? Have you rejoiced at His coming? Do you await His second coming with *joy*? There is so much to look forward to! It should cause our hearts to lift from the ground.

There will always be waves in our experience below, my friend. There will always be something in life to depress and discourage. So, lift up your eyes! Look to the sky. Search for His Star. Locate the King. Fall on your knees. Watch for His coming. And in the here and now, be filled with the *joy* of His salvation, the *joy* of the Holy Spirit, and the *joy* of our bright future with Him.

"Blessed be the God and Father of our Lord Jesus Christ! According to his great mercy, he has caused us to be born again to a living hope ... In this you rejoice, though now for a little while, if necessary, you have been grieved by various trials … Though you do not now see him, you believe in him and *rejoice* with *joy* that is inexpressible and filled with glory" (1 Peter 1:3, 6, 8 ESV, my emphasis added).

> And so here we are, *Awaiting His Coming … Again*!
> Yes, the King has come, and He is coming again!
> May God bless you and be your *joy* this Christmas!
>
> Joy to the world, the Lord is come!
> Let earth receive her King!

DAY

Come and See What God Has Done

Read Matthew 1–2 and Luke 1–2.

Dear Friends,

There is no higher calling for the believer in Jesus Christ than to *worship* Him. This morning, as we trace the events that led to the humble yet extraordinary arrival of God's Son, I am reminded of the invitation presented in Chris Tomlin's Christmas worship song:

> Noel, Noel
> Come and see what God has done
> Noel, Noel
> The story of amazing love!
> The light of the world, given for us
> Noel[4]

Come and see what God has done! Are you too in awe of this story of amazing love? Do your eyes fill with tears when you consider God arriving into our broken world in the humble body of an infant child? Do you ponder and savor all the precious, poignant happenings in the depths of your soul like Mary? Do you search with longing for the Christ like Anna and Simeon? Do you wonder toward the heavens like the magi who came from afar to present their treasures to the King of kings? Do you bow in submission to the will of God like Joseph? Do you bless Him as Lord like Elizabeth? Does your heart leap for joy like those of the shepherds when they received the glorious song of heaven and ran with urgency to find the babe wrapped in swaddling bands, lying in a feeding trough? Do you sink to the ground there as you peer into the human face of God, and worship in awe while beholding the Eternal Father shining in the face of Jesus Christ?

The other day, my small six-year-old daughter wondered to me, "Mommy, when we get to heaven, how will we see God, since God is a Spirit?" I was about to answer her when a gasp of revelation passed through her whole body. She leaped to her feet, eyes shining with light, as she exclaimed to me, "Mommy, I know! Because Jesus is God, when we see Jesus, we will see God!" I was struck with awe at her reply. The incarnation captured in a breath. Christ's deity and humanity grasped in a thought. The purpose of Christ's coming wrapped in a phrase. *When we see Jesus, we will see God.* My child's face was alight with understanding, joy, and dare I say, *worship*? I wish I could have held that holy moment for all eternity. In my heart, I recalled the words of Jesus Himself, when responding to Peter, "Blessed are you ... For flesh and blood has not revealed this to you, but my Father who is in heaven" (Matthew 16:17 ESV). I was amazed at how much the Lord can reveal about His Son and Himself to even a little child of six years of age: "Out of the mouth of babes and nursing infants You have perfected praise" (Matthew 21:16 ESV).

And praise He will perfect! Yes, worshippers He will seek! Whether they be six, sixteen, sixty, or ninety-six. "The time is coming—indeed it's here now—when true worshippers will worship the Father in spirit and in truth. The Father is looking for those who will worship him that way" (John 4:23 NLT). Are you such a worshipper? Am I? Yes, Jesus came to be God with us, to live before us, to die in our place, to rise again for our justification, and to bring us new life. But all these truths are so that we can know Him, love Him, be in relationship with Him, enjoy intimacy with Him, and ultimately, *worship* Him.

You see, my friend, while the world spins through the Christmas season, caught up in Santa Claus and reindeer, toys and tinsel, rum and eggnog, and even though it might tip its hat to a special baby from Bethlehem who grew up to be a good man, a wise teacher, and a fine example for humanity, we, His true worshippers, bend our hearts low to the eternal God of heaven and raise our arms high with praise and gratitude to the Most High, who came as a human baby in the person of our Lord Jesus Christ. We His worshippers acknowledge the truth of His incarnation—all the fullness of God found in a man. We thank Him as our sacrificial Lamb. We honor Him as our Risen Lord, that Lion of Judah. We crown Him as King over all. And we long for His return, so that we may worship Him for all eternity.

Let's start today, friend. Let's be the worshippers the Father is seeking, even now in this Christmas season.

Dear Lord,

Thank You for the precious gift of Your Son, our Lord and Savior, Jesus Christ. Who are we? Who are we to receive such an honor and blessing? May we value Him as You do. May we treasure Him as our own. May we worship Him as we should. We thank You for His first coming, and we long for His second coming, when our worship will be perfected and eternal. In the meantime, we bow our hearts in worship to Your Son in the here and now, while we are …

Awaiting His Coming … Again!
Merry Christmas, everyone!
Love,
Rhoda

Notes

1. Andrew Peterson, "Is He Worthy?," track 13 on *Resurrection Letters, Vol. 1* (Capitol Christian Distribution, 2018).
2. Lauren Daigle, "How Can It Be," track 2 on *How Can It Be* (Centricity Music, 2015), compact disc.
3. C. S. Lewis, *The Lion, the Witch, and the Wardrobe* (New York: Scholastic Inc., 2006).
4. Chris Tomlin, Matt Redman, and Ed Cash, "Noel," track 4 on *Adore: Christmas Songs of Worship* (Sparrow Records, 2015), compact disc.

CPSIA information can be obtained
at www.ICGtesting.com
Printed in the USA
BVHW080219070122
625262BV00001B/3